STUDIES IN THE BRITISH

BUSINESS FINANCE AND THE CITY OF LONDON

STUDIES IN THE BRITISH ECONOMY

General Editor: Derek Lee

Monopoly *by Derek Lee, Vivian Anthony and Allen Skuse*
Regional Planning and the Location of Industry *by Derek Lee*
Britain's Overseas Trade *by Vivian Anthony*
Government Intervention and Industrial Policy *by Allen Skuse*
The Trade Unions *by Hugh Williamson*
Control of the Economy *by Derek Lee*
Banks and Markets *by Vivian Anthony*
National Economic Planning *by Cedric Sandford*
National Income and Expenditure *by Samuel Hays*
The Structure of British Industry *by M. Dunn and P. Tranter*
The Engineering Industries *by Samuel Hays*
The Distributive Trades *by Frank Livesey*
British Population *by R. M. Williams*
The Chemicals and Allied Industries *by Samuel Hays*
The United Kingdom and the World Monetary System *by Brinley Davies*
Britain, the E.E.C. and the Developing World *by M. McQueen*
Pricing in Practice *by J. R. Davies and S. Hughes*
Business Finance and the City of London *by Brinley Davies*
Britain and the European Economic Community *by D. Lewis*
Britain's Agricultural Industry *by Brian Hill*
Investment in the British Economy *by J. R. Davies and S. Hughes*
Trade and Growth *by J. R. Sparkes and C. L. Pass*

STUDIES IN THE BRITISH ECONOMY

Business Finance and the City of London

Second Edition

by
Brinley Davies
Head of Economics,
Worthing Sixth Form College

HEINEMANN EDUCATIONAL
BOOKS LTD · LONDON

Heinemann Educational Books Ltd
22 Bedford Square, London WC1B 3HH
LONDON EDINBURGH MELBOURNE AUCKLAND
HONG KONG SINGAPORE KUALA LUMPUR NEW DELHI
IBADAN LUSAKA NAIROBI JOHANNESBURG
EXETER (NH) KINGSTON PORT OF SPAIN

ISBN 0 435 84579 9

Reproduced, printed and bound in Great Britain by
Cox & Wyman Ltd, London, Fakenham and Reading

CONTENTS

1.	Self-finance and Share Finance	1
2.	Loan Finance	19
3.	Business Finance and the New Issue Market	35
4.	The Workings of the Stock Exchange	48
5.	The Significance of the Stock Exchange	60
6.	Some Criticisms of the London Stock Market	73
7.	The London Stock Market in the 1970s	87
	Appendix A: Preference Shares	111
	Appendix B: Measuring a Share's Performance	113
	Appendix C: A Case Study: the Performance of a Share	116
	Appendix D: Taxation and Business Finance	120
	Appendix E: The Role of the National Enterprise Board	129
	Appendix F: Information for Use in Investment Games	132
	Bibliography	136
	Index	141

PREFACE

Most economics textbooks attempt to cover the subject within a single volume and in consequence some topics are treated briefly: often these same topics are those whose subject matter changes most rapidly. At present in order to keep up to date in the field of economics recourse must be made to a vast field of diffused literature including bank reviews, government publication, newspapers and various journals. With these problems in mind this series was conceived. The series consists of specialized books on those topics which are subject to frequent change or where the sources of information are too scattered to be readily available to the average student. It is intended that each book will be revised at frequent intervals in order to take account of new developments.

PREFACE TO THE SECOND EDITION

In this second edition the scope of the book has been extended. Possible reforms of the London Stock Exchange are examined in the light of its pending investigation by the Office of Fair Trading and against a background of moves in the United States towards an integrated 'national' securities market. A new section of the book examines the 1978 introduction in London of traded options, and the treatment of inflation accounting now includes a comparative discussion of the *current purchasing power* and *current cost accounting* approaches. Finally it has been possible to update the coverage of recent events, including the operation of the National Enterprise Board and the performance of the London stock market in the later 1970s.

1
SELF-FINANCE AND SHARE-FINANCE

Introduction: the role of finance

Finance has been defined as 'provision of money at the time it is wanted'.[1] In this book we shall be examining the way in which firms in the private sector of the economy obtain and use the finance needed to run and expand their operations. A basic aim of these firms is to use their assets, such as machinery and raw materials, so as to earn an income in the form of profit. Now the amount of finance needed to obtain certain assets may be very large. Take the case of a firm wishing to invest in a new and automated production system. Quite possibly, it will find itself needing to pay out considerably more for this than it is currently earning. It may be that it has retained sufficient of its past profits to enable it to finance this new investment. But if this is not the case the firm will need to find someone else willing to provide the finance and will then be required to pay for this finance out of its future earnings. If the firm in question can neither accumulate its own finance nor obtain it externally, it will be forced to limit its investments to its current earnings – and will, for the time being at least, have to go without the new equipment.

It is also important for a firm to ensure that it always has sufficient finance available to meet immediate, and perhaps unforeseen, payments. Otherwise there is a risk that, even if its long-term earning prospects are perhaps quite reasonable, it may find itself unable to meet all its current debts and consequently be declared *insolvent*. It might then be 'put into liquidation' by its creditors – that is, have its assets sold in order to pay off its debts. The more uneven and uncertain a firm's pattern of receipts and payments is, the more important the availability of short-term finance becomes.

Forms of business organization

There are three main types of business organization in the private sector of the economy:

---

[1] F. W. Paish, *Business Finance*, Pitman 1968, page 3.

BUSINESS FINANCE AND THE CITY OF LONDON

1. A *one-man business* (sole proprietorship) is a firm in which one person provides the finance, takes the operating decisions and bears the financial risks involved. This form of business is common, for example, in farming and retailing – its main advantage being that it gives the owner a strong incentive to work hard and efficiently. One drawback, however, is that the owner's financial liability is unlimited — in the event of the firm becoming insolvent all his personal wealth would be at stake to pay its debts. Another snag is that it may be difficult – particularly when taxation is heavy – for one owner to raise, out of the firm's profits or his own personal income and wealth, all the finance needed to run and expand the business. Consequently, one-man businesses often tend to rely heavily on bank finance.

2. A logical development of the one-man business is the *partnership*. This is a firm in which two or more persons (up to a total of twenty) jointly own and control the business. Partnerships are common in many professional services such as accountancy, law, medicine and so on. Two useful advantages of partnerships are that they enlarge the scope for managerial specialization and increase the amount of personal capital which a business is able to draw on. One drawback, however, is that the financial liability of the partners is unlimited (except in the case of *sleeping partners*, who, provided they renounce any part in the running of the firm, are allowed under the Limited Partnerships Act, 1907, to contribute capital on terms of limited liability). Moreover, the acts of any one member may be legally binding on all the other members. Another difficulty with partnerships is that they are terminated by the death or resignation of a partner, thus making necessary new arrangements, including perhaps new membership, to keep their capital structure intact.

3. The most important type of firm in Britain is the *limited joint stock company*. This is a form of business in which the capital is owned by shareholders on the basis of limited liability, obtained generally by company registration under the Companies Acts. The type known as a limited *private* company dates from 1908. A private company must by law have at least two shareholders (but not more than fifty), and is not allowed to issue shares to the general public; nor are its members allowed to transfer shares freely to non-members. At present there are about 500,000 private companies in Britain. A limited *public* company must have at least seven shareholders and is allowed to issue shares to the general public. The amount of capital which a public company may be organized to raise is thus in

principle unlimited. This form of business is therefore in an ideal position to finance the very large investments needed to exploit the economies of scale available in manufacturing industry and certain other sectors of the economy. At the present time there are about 11,000 public companies, and between them they account for about two-thirds of all business activity. In order to safeguard the position of investors, all companies are now required to file annually with the Registrar of Companies, specific information on turnover, profits, assets, liabilities, etc. This takes the form of an annual *balance sheet* (page 6) and *profit and loss account* (page 12).

As public companies now dominate the business scene in Britain they will naturally form the main focus of this book. However we shall also, to the extent that the activities of the City of London affect them, from time to time examine the position of private companies, and smaller firms in general.

Types of external finance

There are two basic types of external finance available to firms. First, there is *borrowing*. Here the firm will be required to pay interest for the finance which it is receiving. If this is for a short period – say, three months – the interest will probably be met at the same time as the loan is repaid. Otherwise, interest is normally paid annually. Bank loans are an important form of borrowing for many firms particularly for shorter periods. However there are a number of other forms, such as finance bills, trade credit, etc (see page 28). In the case of a joint stock company, a key method of borrowing is by issuing securities known as *debentures*. These are, in effect, interest-bearing IOUs, dated for periods up to twenty years or more. Debenture holders are therefore not the owners of a company – they are its creditors. Interest on debentures is a *prior charge* on a company's earnings. That is, it must be paid in full before a company is free to distribute its earnings in any other direction – for example, to shareholders. In the event of a company making losses and eventually being forced out of business, the debenture holders also have a prior claim to the repayment of their capital out of the liquidation of its assets.

Other things being equal, the more certain a firm's earnings prospects are thought to be, the lower will be the rate of interest it is likely to have to offer to obtain loan finance. A well-established bakery or brewery, for example, would normally reckon to be able

3

to borrow more cheaply than, say, a speculative mining firm set up to prospect for a rare mineral.

The second main type of external finance is used by joint stock companies, and consists in issuing securities known as *limited-liability shares*. By *limited liability*, we mean that each shareholder's liability for the debts of the company is limited to the amount which he has invested – he cannot be required to make any further contribution towards meeting the company's debts. The safeguard of limited liability has made it much easier for companies to raise large amounts of capital from investors. Limited liability companies must include the word 'Limited' (or 'Ltd') in their name. Shares represent the ownership of a company and are of two main types. *Ordinary shares* carry the main risks of the business. When a company's profits are high its ordinary shareholders can expect its directors to declare a good dividend on each share, but when profits are low the company is likely to pay little or no dividend. Ordinary shares are often known as *equities*, for they represent a company's equity – that is, what is left over from its earnings when all prior charges on them have been met. Each ordinary share carries one vote in the control of the company. This can be exercised at the annual general meeting of shareholders (in fact, many shareholders do not bother to use their voting rights, unless their company happens to be doing badly and they desire to overthrow the directors). *Preference shares*[1] carry a claim to a certain proportion of the company's profits before the ordinary shareholders receive anything at all. On account of this, preference shares generally carry no voting rights. In the event of a company being put into liquidation, its shareholders stand at the back of the queue for claims on its assets, and if they are unlucky they may receive back little or nothing of their original investment.

In general, the better a company's future profit prospects are believed to be, the lower will be the current dividend which it needs to offer the investing public to persuade it to purchase an issue of its shares. Conversely, a company with a very poor outlook might find it virtually impossible to float any shares.

Setting up a company
When a company is to be formed its promoters are required, under the Companies Acts, to submit to the Registrar of Companies two

---

[1] See Appendix A.

4

important documents. The first is a *Memorandum of Association*, indicating – generally in wide terms to avoid subsequent self-limitation – the purposes for which the company is being formed, and the amount of capital which it may raise. Its *authorized capital* will be formulated in terms of the numbers of shares into which it is divided; for example, an authorized capital of £100,000 might be divided into, say, 200,000 shares of 50 pence nominal value each. However, a company need not necessarily – either initially or later – issue shares to this full extent (although the power will always, so to speak, be in reserve). That is, its *issued capital* may be less than its authorized capital. It should also be noted that a company may not require the full nominal value of its shares to be paid when they are first issued. Thus a company might have an authorized capital of £100,000, an issued capital of £40,000, and a *paid-up capital* of only £20,000 (for example, 25 pence per 50 pence share).

The second document required when a company is formed is its *Articles of Association*, setting out its proposed capital structure (including the various categories of share capital, and the company's borrowing powers), the powers of its directors, and so on. A company's promoters are in addition required to submit to the Registrar a list of directors and their proposed share stake in the company. If all the conditions in the two documents are satisfactorily met, the Registrar of Companies issues a *Certificate of Incorporation* which permits the company in question to commence business as a legal entity, and on a limited-liability basis, on behalf of its shareholders. In the case of a public company it is also necessary, if it has decided to seek a Stock Exchange quotation, to satisfy certain Stock Exchange requirements, which involve filing a *prospectus* outlining the financial position of the company and its future prospects (see page 36).

The growth of a company

Let us continue our examination of business finance by considering the growth of a hypothetical company in terms of its *balance sheet*, which is a statement, for any particular time, of its various assets and liabilities. By an asset we mean what a company 'owns' and by a liability we mean what it 'owes'. Suppose a group of businessmen set up a company to produce a new range of educational toys. They estimate that £60,000 will be needed to buy premises, and another £20,000 for equipment. What are called the company's *fixed assets* (those which do not change hands in the course of production) will therefore amount to £80,000. In addition the company will need to purchase stocks of materials (paper, wood, plastic, and so on) for say £6,000 and hold a safe level of cash in hand for future trading purposes – say, £4,000. The company's *current assets* (those which are turned over regularly) will thus be £10,000. And so its *total assets* will amount to £90,000.

The company in question will thus need to find £90,000 to finance its assets. In principle there are, as explained earlier in this chapter, three main ways in which this can be done: a company can use retained profits; it can borrow – for example by issuing debentures; and it can issue shares. In our example the company, as a new firm, has in fact no past profits to use. We shall therefore, as a simplification, assume that it is able to raise the whole of its finance by the issue of ordinary shares. As the sum in question, £90,000, is a relatively small amount of capital, these shares would be issued privately – in fact it is quite likely that the founding businessmen would themselves take up most, or all, of the share capital. Since the company will, in a sense, be looking after this £90,000 on behalf of its shareholders, the share capital *counts as a company liability*.

If then at this initial stage the company's balance sheet were to be drawn up, it would look like this:

Table 1.1

LIABILITIES	
Share capital	£
90,000 £1 ordinary shares	90,000
	90,000
ASSETS	
Fixed Assets	
Land and buildings	60,000
Machines	20,000
Current Assets	
Stocks	6,000
Cash in hand	4,000
Total Assets	90,000

Suppose that the company succeeded over the next few years in producing an attractive range of toys and making a good profit. We could now stop the film at a later stage and see what had been happening in terms of the company's balance sheet:

Table 1.2

LIABILITIES

Share Capital and Reserve	£	£
90,000 £1 ordinary shares	90,000	
Reserve	12,500	
Total		102,500
Current Liabilities		
Creditors	37,000	
Current taxation	16,500	
Proposed dividends	3,000	
		56,500
		159,000

ASSETS

Fixed Assets (after allowing for depreciation)

	£
Land and buildings	60,000
Machines	37,500
Goodwill	3,000
Total	100,500
Current Assets	
Stocks	21,000
Debtors	32,500
Cash in hand	5,000
	58,500
	159,000

Looking first at the assets section of the balance sheet we can see that the company's fixed assets have, even after allowing for machinery *depreciation* (that is, wear-and-tear), expanded, from £80,000 to £100,500. This includes extra machines and also a new asset which has appeared – the item *goodwill*, at £3,000. In general terms, goodwill arises when one firm acquires another firm's assets for more than their book value, on account of patents, expertise and other intangible advantages tied up with their use. Excess payments of this kind are entered in the balance sheet in the form of an asset known as goodwill.

We can see, too, that the company's current assets have increased, from £10,000 to £58,000, this new amount being made up of stocks, cash in hand, and the various trade debts which the company is now owed in the course of its everyday business (the asset called *debtors*). Thus, taking both fixed and current assets together, the company's total assets now stand at £159,000.

The company's total liabilities have also correspondingly increased. Part of the new total consists of *current liabilities*, at £56,500, in the form of (i) trade debts to other firms (*creditors*) (ii) *current taxation* of profits and (iii) *proposed dividends* to shareholders (dividends which are, so to speak, being looked after by the company until they are actually paid out). A second element of increased liabilities consists of depreciation funds which the company has been putting aside out of its earnings to finance the replacement of its fixed assets as they wear out. Depreciation funds need not necessarily be kept in cash or a liquid form at all – in fact it is common for companies to plough back these funds as they become available into further fixed assets. The remaining liability in the balance sheet is the *reserve* of £12,500 which the company has been able to put aside out of its profits, after payment of tax and the distribution of dividends. Since these retained profits really 'belong' to its shareholders, the company's reserve is shown in the balance sheet as a liability. The uses to which the reserve has been put will of course be reflected in the assets section of the balance sheet – for example, machinery, stocks etc.

Retained finance

The balance sheet which we have just been examining introduced us to an important category of business finance, namely *retained finance*. A company's capacity to generate internal finance over a given period is measured by its *cash flow*, which consists of accumulated depreciation allowances plus undistributed profits. Other things being equal, the higher a company's cash flow is, the less it will need to use external finance.

1. Depreciation funds

Taking depreciation finance first, a company's fixed assets are regarded as they depreciate, as continually yielding up part of their value in the output being produced. In order to take account of this erosion of productive capacity, and to enable the level of fixed assets to be maintained, it is usual for companies to set aside funds at a defined rate in the form of a *depreciation allowance* against fixed assets. Since the depreciation of fixed assets can legitimately be regarded as a cost of production, that part of a company's annual revenue which is used for depreciation is not considered a part of its profits, nor subject to taxation.

In calculating its depreciation requirements, it is first necessary for a company to decide the likely useful life of the asset in question. The greater this is, the less revenue will need to be set aside annually. Secondly, it is necessary to estimate at what rate the asset is likely to lose its value as a productive factor, both on account of physical wear-and-tear and of *obsolescence* – that is, the fact that it may be becoming out-of-date compared with more modern equipment. Two main methods of depreciation are used. One is the *straight-line* depreciation method. Take the case of some new equipment which is purchased by a company for £10,000 and which has an estimated life of ten years. Using the straight-line depreciation method it would be assumed that the equipment was worth £9,000 after one year, £8,000 after two years, £7,000 after three years, and ultimately zero after ten years. The company would therefore set aside £1,000 annually in its accounts to enable the equipment to be replaced when it came to the end of its life. In the *reducing balance* depreciation method, on the other hand, a fixed asset is assumed to lose value most rapidly in its early years and least rapidly towards the end of its life. A constant percentage of the machine's current value at each stage of its life is accordingly deducted each year. Thus, if, in our example, the rate used was 20 per cent, the amount set aside for depreciation in the first year would be £2,000 (20 per cent of £10,000). In the second year it would be £1,600 (20 per cent of £8,000), and so on.

When the time comes for a fixed asset finally to be scrapped or sold, any proceeds are recorded in the company's profit and loss account (see p. 12). If scrapping takes place before the asset is fully depreciated, the proceeds are compared with its remaining written down value and the resulting loss or profit is then transferred to the profit and loss account.

In general, the British tax authorities allow depreciation rates of around 20 per cent on plant, and an estimated life of up to 15 years or more. If a company wishes to set aside more than this agreed rate (for example so as to be able to replace plant more quickly and so keep abreast of technical developments) it is free to do so – but will get no tax relief on the difference.

Although it is clearly essential for a company to earmark a specific part of its annual revenue to cover depreciation, the actual way in which it uses these funds is open to choice. A company might for example keep them as a bank deposit, invest them in central or local government securities, or use them to finance stocks of raw materials or to reduce its current debts. Again, the funds might be used immediately to purchase new and possibly quite different, fixed assets – as in the case of depreciation funds generated by a British paper-making firm being re-invested by the parent company in Australian vineyards. In other words, depreciation funds are simply part of a company's overall cash flow, and may be used accordingly as its directors think fit.

A final factor which we need to examine is the effect on depreciation requirements of changing prices. If, while depreciation funds are being put aside during the working life of an asset, the general level of prices falls, the company in question will have funds left over when a new, cheaper asset is purchased to replace the old one. It will thus have received an unplanned tax-free addition to its profits. Conversely, a rising price level will, given traditional accounting practices (see p. 92), mean that depreciation funds tend to be inadequate to replace fixed assets at new and higher prices; the shortfall will thus have to come out of a company's taxed profits. This important point is considered further in Chapter 7.

2. Retained profits

The other main source of retained finance consists of accumulated profits which, in most periods, have been the main source of expansion funds for British companies. One factor affecting a company's position in this respect is its policy on dividend distributions. Clearly, the more it is prepared to limit dividends, the more profit will remain available for ploughing back into its operations. Moreover, some managements are apparently influenced by the (incorrect) belief that retained earnings somehow constitute free finance, compared with the alternative of expensive external finance.[1] However there are definite limitations on the ability of a company to pursue a high retention and low dividend policy. One is the fact that low dividends make it difficult for a company to induce investors to take up new share issues, should this at any time prove necessary. There is also the associated risk that a company's existing shareholders may become restless, though experience shows that unless dividends are extremely poor it is rare for shareholders to unseat a board of direc-

---

[1] R. J. Briston, *The Stock Exchange and Investment Analysis*, George Allen and Unwin, p. 130.

tors. Another limitation is that low dividends may result in a low market price for a company's shares and so increase the risk of take-over bids by rival companies wishing to acquire its assets on the cheap (see p. 64).

Secondly, the role of retained profits depends upon the size of a company's earnings. The higher these are, the greater will be its ability (other things, including investment plans, being equal) to finance a substantial part of its operations from its own resources. It turns out, in fact, that the broad trend of profitability of companies in Britain has for many years been falling. The causes of this decline are far from fully understood (see Chapter 7 for some suggested reasons). What is significant in our present context however is that the effect of lower profits has been to reduce the ability of companies to generate internal finance. In recent years companies have been driven to rely increasingly on external loan finance, particularly from the banking system or from official or semi-official agencies such as Finance for Industry (p. 105) and the proposed National Enterprise Board (p. 129).

A third factor has been the amount of *corporation tax* which companies have been required to pay on their profits (Appendix D, p. 122). In recent years this has been as high as 52 per cent and, in spite of investment allowances and grants (p. 127) heavy taxation has increased the financial pressures on many companies.

The use of company accounts for assessing share prospects
We saw earlier that a basic motive for the purchase of a share is the expectation of receiving a dividend income out of the profits of the company in question. There are however many investors for whom the income motive is reinforced by the motive of capital growth, by which we mean an expectation of increasing profits and dividends, *and consequently a rising market value*, for the share in question. The other side of the growth coin however is risk. As we have seen, ordinary share dividends come at the back of the queue as a claim on a company's earnings, and are paid – if at all – only after interest on debentures (and other loan capital), corporation tax, and pre-ference share dividends have all been met. The risk element for ordinary shares can be seen most clearly in the case of a company which is in a line of business where profits are uncertain and fluctuate considerably. When profits are high, shareholders will be likely, when tax and debt interest have been paid, to receive good dividends. But

11

when profits are low, or actual losses are being made, the share-holders may receive nothing at all.

Much of the basic information needed to assess the prospects for a share is to be found in a company's two sets of financial accounts, namely its balance sheet and its *profit and loss account*. A very useful summary in these respects for every quoted company is provided in the *Stock Exchange Official Year Book*, which is a standard reference work. As we saw on p. 6, a company balance sheet shows, for a particular moment in time, the state of its assets and liabilities. It thus sums up, as it were, a company's past history. A profit and loss account, on the other hand, gives a picture of how a company is currently running, in terms of its costs, turnover, profits and other operating factors. Each profit and loss account is based on a company's most recent accounting year, and is divided into three main parts:

1. *The trading account*. This shows, (i) the company's *turnover*: that is, the revenue received from the goods and services which it has sold over the past year; and (ii) its operating expenses. The difference between a company's turnover and total operating costs is called its *trading profit*.

2. *The profit and loss account*. This converts a company's trading profit into a clean *net profit*. First it is necessary to deduct a number of prior charges which a company has to meet out of its trading profit, including directors' and auditors' fees, staff pension funds, and interest on debentures and other loan capital. This leaves us with the company's *gross profit before tax*. Next, depreciation funds which have been set aside during the year must be subtracted to give the *net profit before tax* of the company. Finally, subtracting from this the amount of corporation tax at the current rate gives the company's *net profit after tax*.

3. *The appropriation account*. This shows how a company has used (that is, appropriated) the past year's net profit after tax. One important appropriation usually consists of dividends to the share-holders; another is the amount of profit retained by the company. In the case of a loss, the account shows which funds have been used to meet the loss. Here is an example of a profit and loss account, which is related to information in the toy company's balance sheets shown earlier in this chapter (it is assumed as a simplification that the interval of time between the two balance sheets is only one year).

Table 1.3

TRADING ACCOUNT	£	£
Turnover		171,000
Operating expenses		130,000

PROFIT AND LOSS ACCOUNT		
Trading profit		41,000
Directors' fees	1,500	
Auditors' fees	250	
Staff pensions	750	
Depreciation (20% of machine value)	7,500	
Interest on loan capital	nil	
		10,000
Net profit before tax		31,000
Corporation Taxation at (say) 50%		15,500
Net profit after tax		15,500

APPROPRIATION ACCOUNT		
Earned for ordinary shares		15,500
Ordinary dividend		3,000
		12,500
Transferred to reserves		12,500

A company's profit and loss accounts and balance sheets for recent years can be used as a guide to its future performance in terms of profits and share dividends. One key factor is the amount of profit which the company has been earning in recent years – the higher this is, the better. However, if the company's assets have not also been expanding significantly, its profits may well eventually level off. One reason for this is that there is likely to be a limit to the ability of any management to continue squeezing more and more efficiency, and profits, out of a given level of assets. Secondly, there is the likelihood that a very high return on capital (what economists call supra-normal profit) may eventually attract competition from other firms, and lead to pressures on profit levels. Suppose, however, a company's accounts show that although its total profits have been rising, its assets and turnover have been increasing even faster, so that the rate of return on its invested capital has actually been declining. Clearly, the future outlook for such a company would not be very promising. It follows that the prospects for profits and dividends will tend to be

13

best where a company's use of assets and rate of return on them are both increasing together.[1] A good case in point would be the highly successful development of the Tesco food store chain in the 1960s[2] (see Appendix C).

Company accounts are also used to gauge the likely impact of constantly changing economic circumstances on future earnings – as for example, in 1974, when many companies' profits were under pressure from a number of directions. On the side of costs, there were at this time higher interest rates and wages, dearer oil, and the effects of the emergency three-day working week.[3] On the side of turnover, an important factor was that of government price controls on companies. The reader who wishes to see how these factors were assessed in terms of their likely effects on companies' profitability, should consult the specialist financial press for the period in question (see Bibliography).

Share prospects and capital structure

Another factor affecting a share's prospects is not just how much profit a company is likely to be earning, but also how its operations are to be financed. What we are referring to here is a company's *capital structure*, which can affect the way in which its earnings are distributed among the owners of different classes of security. When a company has a high ratio of fixed-return capital to ordinary-share capital, we say it has a *high capital gearing*. When this ratio is low we speak of a *low capital gearing*.

Take the case of a completely *ungeared* company, whose operations have been based entirely on £1 million of share capital, earning £200,000 of profit annually (that is, an earnings rate of 20 per cent). Suppose it now raises £500,000 of debenture capital, at 12 per cent, and yet continues to earn 20 per cent on its expanded operations. Clearly, its shareholders would benefit from this differential, for of the £300,000 now being earned, only £60,000 would be needed to pay debenture interest, which would leave £240,000 available for the ordinary shareholders – representing an earnings rate of 24 per cent on the company's ordinary share capital. A further debenture issue of, say, £1½ million at 12 per cent, would increase this *gearing effect*

[1] J. Rowlatt and D. Davenport, *Guide to Savings and Investment*, David and Charles, 1971, p. 72.
[2] Ibid.
[3] See Chapter 7.

still further, and allow the earnings rate on its share capital to rise to 36 per cent. (See table 1.4).

Suppose it turned out, though, that the company's rate of return on its invested capital was lower than expected – say only 8 per cent. The damaging effect of this in a highly geared situation can be seen in table 1.4.

Table 1.4

| | CAPITAL STRUCTURE | | |
	ungeared	*low-geared*	*high-geared*
Ordinary shares	1,000,000	1,000,000	1,000,000
12% debentures	—	500,000	2,000,000
Total capital employed	1,000,000	1,500,000	3,000,000
20% profit on capital	200,000	300,000	600,000
Interest on debentures	—	60,000	240,000
Available for 'ordinary'	200,000	240,000	360,000
Earnings rate on ordinary capital	20%	24%	36%
8% profit on capital	80,000	120,000	240,000
Interest on debentures	—	60,000	240,000
Available for 'ordinary'	80,000	60,000	nil
Earnings rate on ordinary capital	8%	6%	nil

Other things being equal, the effect of a highly geared capital structure is clearly to increase fluctuations in a company's equity earnings, and thus the degree of risk faced by its ordinary share-holders. (The reader will be able to confirm this by extending table 1.4 so as to show the effect of a rise in profitability to 30 per cent, compared with the original level.)

The point we are considering can also be extended to include the effect of a company's future commitments for capital expenditure. If these are substantial a highly geared capital structure may result, which increases the vulnerability of shareholders to changes in profits. Alternatively, the extra finance needed may take the form mainly of new shares, including rights issues (see p. 41). Even here, though, until the investment programme finally has paid off in higher profits, earnings per share might tend to be reduced (diluted).

The Stock Exchange and business finance

When public companies issue securities they employ the services of firms known as *issuing houses* and *underwriters* which operate on the *primary* securities market known as the *new issue market*. The working of the new issue market is however supported by the activity of the *secondary* securities market – that is, the Stock Exchange. The main Stock Exchange is in London, but there are a number of provincial exchanges in Birmingham, Liverpool and other centres, which are now closely linked to the London Stock Exchange. The operation of the Stock Exchange revolves around the activities of two types of dealer. First, there are numbers of competing *jobbers* who hold, or can obtain, securities on their own behalf – they are, as it were, wholesalers in securities. Secondly, there are the stock *brokers*, who act as agents for the investing public by placing their orders with the jobbers.

It should be stressed that the Stock Exchange does not constitute a direct mechanism for the raising of new capital for companies. Its importance lies in the fact that, by giving investors an assurance that any company securities which they purchase will be marketable, it provides a back-up role for the new issue market. In theory, a new issue market might manage to operate up to a point even if there was no Stock Exchange. For one thing there might be a market in unofficial dealings, such as those which take place alongside the present Stock Exchange arrangements. However if an unofficial market did not exist, the position of investors (and of companies wishing to draw on their savings) would be a very difficult one. For once an investor had purchased a company security he might, in the absence of a secondary securities market, find it very difficult to turn his investment back into cash. (Perhaps he would advertise in the agony column of *The Times*, buttonhole his friends at the golf club, or hold an auction at the village hall!) And the price which he obtained for his securities, even if he could find a buyer, would be unpredictable and perhaps very disappointing. This could be particularly important when, on a person's death, private wealth in the form of securities needed to be sold for inheritance or to pay for estate duty. It should also be noted that people who invest in new issues frequently obtain the funds to pay for them by marketing some of their existing holdings of securities on the Stock Exchange. Summing up, then, if there were not an efficient stock market, it is doubtful whether investors would be prepared to supply much capital to companies through the new issue market.

Another feature of the Stock Exchange is that it has a Council, consisting of members chosen by ballot, whose function is to ensure honest business standards on the London capital market. Apart from vetting the standing of companies wishing to use the capital market, the Council also has powers to suspend or otherwise discipline dealers who by rigging the market, or by exploiting confidential inside knowledge, attempt to make an unfair profit at the expense of other investors. The Stock Exchange also operates a *compensation fund*, levied on members and designed to protect investors in the event of a dealer going bankrupt (this fund was in fact used a number of times in the dark days of 1974).

It must not be assumed, of course, that the Stock Exchange works perfectly, or cannot be improved. In fact it has recently come in for a considerable amount of criticism (see Chapter 6). Enough has been said however to show that the Stock Exchange is not a mere gambling shop and that it does have a useful part to play in the raising of business finance.

Conclusion: the allocation of share finance resources

A company which, on the evidence of its accounts, is being operated efficiently and profitably will generally be able to raise share capital more easily and cheaply than a less successful company would. As it becomes able to pay higher dividends out of its expanding profits, an increased demand will develop for its shares on the stock market, with the result that the shares' market price rises. In fact, investors in this situation are often prepared to bid up the market price of the share in question extremely high. That is to say, they are prepared to accept a low *current* market dividend yield (see p. 113), in the expectation of receiving greatly increased dividends from the company's *future* expansion of profits.

To take a simplified example, imagine that a company decided to expand by going public, on the basis of an expected annual profit available for dividends of £80,000. If investors had great confidence in its future capacity to increase its profits, they might be prepared to purchase its shares at a current dividend of only, say, 2 per cent. The company in question would therefore be able, on the basis of its expected £80,000 dividend, to raise about £4 million of share capital from investors.

17

Conversely, another company, also currently earning £80,000 of distributable profits, but with apparently much less promising prospects, might in order to float its shares have to offer investors a much higher dividend – say 8 per cent. It would then be able only to raise £1 million, compared with the £4 million available to its more successful rival; in which case it might decide to postpone, or abandon, its expansion plans.

It must be stressed, though, that there are some important qualifications which need to be made to this rather simplified picture:

1. The interpretation of company performance in terms of published accounts is an inexact and subjective procedure (see p. 73). Hence the investor attitudes which determine a share's dividend yield may be ill-founded, and turn out mistaken.

2. It is disputed by some economists whether a company's profit record in the past can even in principle be relied upon as an indicator of its future performance! (see p. 83).

3. The discussion above is valid only if it is assumed that share prices represent a neutral and balanced market assessment of a company's prospects and that they are not distorted by erratic speculative pressures (see p. 53) or by an unduly pessimistic or optimistic general mood on the stock market (see p. 101).

2
LOAN FINANCE

Introduction
We saw in Chapter 1 that a company has open to it a number of possible sources of finance, namely:

1. Self-finance, consisting of accumulating depreciation funds and retained profits which together constitute a company's 'cash flow'.
2. Share-finance, via the issue to investors of limited liability shares, either privately or on the open market.
3. Loan finance, which may in turn be subdivided into
   (a) Long-term loan finance, notably debenture capital, but also including longer-term bank finance and certain other specialized sources.
   (b) Short-term loan finance, in the form of bank credit, finance bills, trade credit, etc.

We shall begin this chapter on loan finance by looking at debentures.

The role of debentures
Debentures are, as we have seen, long-dated interest-bearing IOUs, issued by companies for specified periods of up to twenty years or more. Debentures carry a fixed rate of interest which a company is legally obliged to pay, regardless of how satisfactory its current trading position may happen to be. If a company is unable to pay this interest fully, its debenture holders, as creditors, have the right to appoint a *receiver* who may in the final resort put the company into liquidation. The proceeds from the sale of its assets will then be used towards paying debenture holders' back-interest, together with the capital which is owed them. Thus a company wishing to issue debentures needs to be satisfied both that its future earnings are likely to be reasonably stable and that its assets are readily marketable. Debentures may, once they have been issued, be bought and sold second-hand on the Stock Exchange: a facility which enhances their attractiveness to investors.

In Chapter 1 we looked at self-finance and share-finance in terms of a hypothetical company's balance sheets and profit and loss accounts. In this chapter we shall be using a similar method for studying debenture finance. We shall begin by supposing that the company's directors decide, at some stage after we last left them (see tables 1.2 and 1.3) to put up extra buildings costing £50,000. In view of its good profit record the company is now able to find this sum by issuing debentures at an interest rate of, say, 9 per cent. When our company had issued the debentures and purchased its new premises, the balance sheet of its expanded operations might now look like this:

Table 2.1

LIABILITIES	£	£
Share Capital and Reserve		
90,000 £1 ordinary shares	90,000	
Reserve	33,000	
Total		123,000
Loan Capital		
9% debenture stock		50,000
Future Taxation		11,000
Current Liabilities		
Creditors	21,000	
Current Taxation	25,000	
Proposed dividends	5,000	
		51,000
		235,000

ASSETS		
Fixed Assets (net of depreciation)		
Land and buildings	110,000	
Machines	54,000	
Goodwill	3,000	
Total		167,000
Current Assets		
Stocks	23,000	
Debtors	31,000	
Cash in hand	14,000	
		68,000
		235,000

Assessing the prospects for a debenture

Investment in ordinary shares is, as we saw earlier, associated with the ideas of growth and risk. In the case of debentures we find that the main investment motive is not uncertain growth but secure income. It follows that the prospects for any given debenture depend on three main requirements:

1. The assets of the company concerned should be likely to maintain their value and be readily marketable. If then for any reason it should be forced out of business, the repayment of the debenture capital and any back-interest will not be in danger.
2. The earnings of the company should be sufficiently steady from one year to another to cover the annual interest payments due to its debenture holders.
3. The terms of the debenture issue should adequately protect the position of the debenture holders as creditors.

We shall now consider these three points in turn.

Capital cover for debentures

The greater the estimated market value of a company's assets, the more secure, other things being equal, will be the position of the debenture holders. A key concept in this connection is that of *net tangible assets*. This is meant to measure the present *real value* of a company's assets, and show the financial backing available in the last resort to repay the debenture holders' capital. Net tangible assets are calculated from data available in the company balance sheet, in the following way:

1. Current liabilities are subtracted from current assets to give the value of the company's *net current assets*; this is often known as its *working capital*.
2. To this figure is added the value of the company's total fixed assets.
3. Certain *intangible* assets in the balance sheet, notably goodwill, (see p. 7) are then deducted. It is of course true that if the company's judgement has been sound the purchase of the goodwill should turn out to have been worthwhile. But if the company goes out of business and is forced to sell its assets, it is by no means certain that any other firm would be interested in purchasing the goodwill from it. So to be on the safe side goodwill is deducted.
4. *Deferred liabilities*, such as future tax payments, are deducted.

Table 2.2 is an example of the calculations involved, based on the balance sheet above. It can be seen that the company's £50,000 of debenture capital is backed by £170,000 of real assets.

Table 2.2		£	£
	Current assets	68,000	
Minus	current liabilities	51,000	
	Net current assets		17,000
Plus	total fixed assets	167,000	
Minus	goodwill	3,000	
			164,000
			181,000
Minus	deferred tax liabilities		11,000
	Net tangible assets		170,000

Unfortunately, the figure for a company's net tangible assets as estimated in practice is often far from reliable:

1. The valuation of land and buildings as entered in a company's balance sheet is generally either at their original *historical* cost or when they were last valued – which may have been many years earlier. Since that time their value as capital cover for debentures may have increased greatly and this ought to be taken into account in calculating the net tangible assets. Some extra information on this point is usually to be found in the *supplementary notes* to a company's balance sheet.

2. A second snag arises from the distinction between the value of a company's assets as a going concern, and their possibly much reduced break-up value if it were to go out of business. It is not however possible to assess accurately the latter from the company's balance sheet – particularly in the case of highly specific plant whose re-sale value might be very little indeed compared with its book value.

Since however factor 1 tends to underestimate the value of fixed assets and factor 2 tends to exaggerate their value, then, as a rough working compromise, the break-up value of a company's fixed assets as a whole is sometimes taken to be approximately equal to their book value in the balance sheet.

Capital structure and debenture cover
The cover for a company's debentures is also reflected in its capital

structure. As we saw on page 14, when a company has a high proportion of fixed-return capital (that is, preference shares and debentures) to share capital, it is said to have a 'high capital gearing'. When the ratio of fixed-return capital to share capital is low we say the company has a 'low capital gearing'. Let us now consider a low-geared company which has net tangible assets of £1,000,000, which have been financed as in table 2.3.

Table 2.3

Class of capital	£	%
5% debentures	100,000	10
9% debentures	40,000	4
6% preference	110,000	11
Ordinary and reserve	750,000	75
Total	1,000,000	100

The *capital cover* would then be calculated as follows:

Table 2.4

Class of capital	%	Capital priority percentages	Over-all cover
5% debentures	10	0–10	10·0 times
9% debentures	4	10–14	7·1 times
6% preference	11	14–25	4·0 times
Ordinary and reserve	75	25–100	

It can be seen that three-quarters of the company's capital has been provided by the shareholders, whilst the class of 5 per cent debentures, by contrast, represents only one-tenth of the company's capital. The 5 per cent debenture holders are thus concentrated at the very front of the queue, with a *capital priority percentage* of 0–10. This means that the first 10 per cent only of the company's asset value would be needed to repay the 5 per cent debentures. Their capital cover is thus ten times. Putting the point another way, if the company's assets, on being sold, were to realize only one-tenth of their book value, the 5 per cent debenture holders could still be repaid their capital in full – though the remaining classes of securities would then receive nothing.

Similarly, the 9 per cent debenture holders, with a capital priority percentage of 10–14, have a claim on the next 4 per cent of the company's assets, and are thus covered on capital 7·1 times. Finally, the preference share capital has a claim on the next 11 per cent of the assets; it is therefore covered exactly four times on capital.

It can be seen that the greater the capital cover for debentures, the more secure their repayment would be in the event of the company going into liquidation. Conversely, a debenture which was only, say, twice-covered on capital, might be very vulnerable in the event of liquidation. For if the company's assets, on being sold, were to realize anything less than half their book value, it would be impossible for the debenture holders to be fully repaid the capital which they had lent the company.

Income cover for debentures

Turning next to what is termed *income cover* for debentures, we have already indicated that the key requirement is not that a company's trading profits should necessarily be growing rapidly, but rather that they should as far as possible be steady from one year to the next so that the debenture interest can be paid even when the trading profit is at its lowest. This in turn relates to what is called a company's *income gearing*. When a company's debenture interest and preference dividends (that is, its prior charges) constitute only a small claim on its trading profits, we say that it has a *low* income gearing. Consider, for example, table 2.5, which is based on the figures in the preceding section, and assumes that the company in question is making an annual profit of £50,000.

Table 2.5

	Cost of interest or dividend	Income priority percentage	Income cover
£100,000 of 5% debentures	£2,750*	0–5·5	18·2 times
£40,000 9% debentures	£1,980*	5·5–9·5	10·5 times
£110,000 6% preference	£6,600	9·5–22·7	4·4 times
Ordinary and reserve	£38,670	72·7–100	—

 * Net cost, due to 45% corporation tax relief.[1]

We can see that the 5 per cent debenture interest, at £2750, amounts to only 5·5 per cent of the company's profits; it therefore has an income cover of 18·2 times. Similarly the 8 per cent debenture interest has a claim on the next 4 per cent slice of the profits, and is safely

---

[1] See p. 117.

covered 10·5 times. The preference dividend, at 4·4 times is itself quite well covered, reflecting the fact that, following on from the claims of the debenture interest, it pre-empts a relatively small further percentage of the company's profits. It is apparent then that the profits of the company shown in table 2.5 could fall substantially without putting at risk either the debenture interest or the preference dividend.

Contrast this however with the situation shown in table 2.6.

Table 2.6

	Cost of interest or dividend	Income priority percentage	Income cover
£300,000 of 5% debentures	£8,250*	0–15·5	6·45 times
£120,000 9% debentures	£5,940*	15·5–28·5	3·51 times
£330,000 6% preference	£19,800	28·5–68·1	1·47 times
Ordinary and reserve	£17,010	68·1–100	

* Net cost, due to 45 per cent corporation tax relief.[1]

The company in question has evidently at some stage in the past raised a large amount of debenture and preference capital, the interest and dividends of which now constitute a heavy claim on its profits. It therefore has a *high* income gearing. The reader will see that should its profits fall by, say, one-half, to £25,000, the preference dividend could not be fully paid. Whilst a fall in profits of three-quarters to £12,500 would not only cause the preference interest to cease, but would even curtail the 9 per cent debenture interest. We are assuming that the company had adopted the practice of ranking new debenture issues below existing debentures, so that the holders of the most recent debentures would bear the brunt of the reduced interest payments. If the company were one in which new issues of debentures are given an equal ranking with existing debentures, all the debenture holders would then suffer equally any reduced interest payments which might be necessary. Either way, it would be no consolation that the preference and ordinary shareholders would receive no dividend at all.

The more irregular and uncertain a company's earnings are, the more unsafe it is for it to pursue a high-gearing policy based on raising large amounts of priority capital. In practice – though this

[1] See p. 117.

obviously depends on the type of industry in question – the minimum income cover considered safe for debentures is generally about five times. The corresponding minimum capital cover (see p. 23) for debentures is generally considered to be about four times – rather lower, for a company is much more likely at some time or other to go through some lean trading years than to go out of business altogether. In order to protect debenture holders against the risk of over-gearing, the maximum amount of loan capital, including debentures, which a company may raise is generally specified in its memorandum or articles of association. For example, it might be stated that the total loan capital must not exceed one half of the company's share capital.

The repayment of debenture capital

Since the debenture holders have no say in the general running of a company, it is desirable for their interests to be protected by means of specific provisions for the eventual repayment of the debenture capital. This may be done by the company putting aside every year a fixed sum in the form of a *sinking fund* with which it can in due course repay the debenture capital. Alternatively, a company may finance the repayment of one class of debentures by floating a new issue of debentures. The snag here, from the company's point of view, is that the rate of interest may happen to be much higher than when the earlier issue of debentures was made. Thirdly, a company may, in the event of its debentures falling to a low market price, buy them back piecemeal from their existing holders out of its profits – it will then (in effect) be transforming its debenture capital into share capital.

Debenture holders also need protection in the event of the company going out of business. We saw above that a good basic protection is afforded when the company's net tangible assets have a high value. More specifically however it is common for debentures to be secured as a *direct charge* against particular assets of the company. Where these consist of fixed assets, such as land and buildings, we speak of a *mortgage debenture*. If they are the company's current assets, we use the term *floating charge debenture*. Since mortgage debenture holders know precisely what assets are available as capital cover, this type of debenture can usually be issued at a rather lower rate of interest than floating debentures. Finally, it is useful in practice for the security of the debentures to be tied to a *trustee* (for example, an insurance company or a bank) which can then represent the debenture holders as a group in the event of the company running into difficulties.

Shares and debentures: a comparison

Both debentures and shares are securities issued by companies to raise finance – but there the similarity ends. The main differences are as follows:

1. Debenture holders, as creditors of a company, have no say in its running operations (except in the case of possible liquidation). Shareholders, on the other hand, are owners and members of a firm and have (in theory, at least) a controlling say in its operations.

2. Debentures are a fixed-return security, whereas shares are a variable-return security, on which the dividends paid (if any) depend on the level of the company's profits.

3. If a company makes losses and eventually goes bankrupt, the shareholders are likely to find themselves holding a security with little or no market value, since they stand at the very end of the queue for claims on the assets of the company. Debentures, on the other hand, rank as a prior claim against a company's assets. Moreover debenture capital must be repaid (redeemed) by a specified date (although the company may reserve the right to opt for an earlier repayment if it finds this convenient).

4. The interest which a company pays to its debenture holders counts as an allowable expense for tax purposes. This means that if corporation tax is around 45 per cent, a company paying interest at, say 12 per cent on its debentures, needs to find, in terms of profits, the equivalent of only about 7 per cent. Dividend payments on the other hand attract no tax relief, since the shareholders are regarded as being members of the company in question.

Other forms of long-term loan finance

Debentures, although of key importance, are not the only form of long-term loan finance used by firms. Traditionally, on account of their short-term obligations to their depositors, banks in Britain have been reluctant to make long-term loans to firms. However, in practice they do to a considerable extent lend long – particularly to smaller firms which are unable to raise external finance through shares or debentures. Many short-term bank loans are often in practice more or less automatically renewed at intervals and become in effect long-term finance. However they are no substitute for genuine long-term finance at fixed interest rates and for specific periods of 20 years or more. More recently, however, the banks have started to make explicit long-term loans to firms. For example, the Midland Bank's term loan scheme, which started in 1959, was especially designed to provide for small firms' fixed capital requirements. The ceiling for loans under the scheme was fixed at about £10,000 and their duration from three to five years in the case of plant, and up to ten years or more in the case of premises. There are also a number of specialized institutions which make available long-term finance for firms, such as the ICFC and IFC (see p. 32) and Finance for Industry (p. 105).

The allocation of loan-finance resources

We saw in Chapter 1 that a company which had been operating efficiently and profitably would probably be able to raise share capital on the open market more cheaply and easily than its competitors. The same point applies to loan-finance: it will tend to go to those companies which in the view of investors, and on the evidence of their past record, seem most likely to use it effectively. Moreover, this will be enhanced by the trend of second-hand debenture prices on the Stock Exchange. Thus the debentures of a company with a good steady profit record, and a high level of net tangible assets, would be highly regarded by investors and therefore have a relatively high market price, and hence low market yield. This would enable it to raise new debenture finance at a low rate of interest, compared with other companies. Conversely, the debentures of a company which had been using its assets inefficiently and unprofitably would have a low market price. Hence it would need to offer a higher rate of interest to raise debenture finance – assuming it was advisable for it to try. It should be noted, however, that since debentures occupy a much more secure claim in a company's earnings than do shares the spread of interest rates on quoted debentures is likely to be much less than the spread of dividend yields between different shares.

Short-term loan finance

In addition to satisfying their long-term capital needs, it is also important for firms to have access to short-term finance when necessary. For a firm which is running at a good profit over the longer run may still find itself at a particular moment in a tight cash flow position – for example, due to a temporary fall in sales revenue, combined with an increase in money tied up in stocks. It will then need short-term finance for, say, a few months, in order to bridge the gap between its payments and receipts. There are several sources of short-term finance:

1. *Trade credit*. As we saw earlier (p. 7) a firm is likely in the course of its everyday operations to find itself owing money to, and being owed money by, other firms for purchases and sales not yet settled in cash. The net amounts involved for a particular firm may be quite large and so provide a substantial element of short-term finance. Trade credit is, however, an expensive form of finance, for the borrower is likely to lose the cash discounts which firms generally grant to customers for immediate payment of a trade account.

2. *Bank credit*. Apart from the longer-term finance mentioned above, the commercial banks also provide many firms with substantial amounts of short-term finance for working capital. This may be in the form of a bank *overdraft*, whereby the borrowing firm pays interest only on the outstanding debt at any particular time – a convenient form for a firm whose short-term finances fluctuate a great deal. The other form is that of a fixed *loan* for a specific period, say six months: this will often turn out to be more expensive than an overdraft since the borrowing firm will from time to time probably be paying for unused credit facilities.

3. *Bills of exchange*. These are, in effect, short-dated IOUs issued for a specific period (typically, three or six months), at the end of which the bill is redeemed, and the loan thus repaid[1]. The main type of bill of exchange was once the *trade* bill, used by firms to obtain bridging finance, while waiting for goods to be sold. Nowadays efficient international banking has led to the decline of the trade bill, and the main type of bill of exchange is now the *finance bill*. Here no trade is directly involved and the bill represents direct finance from the institution buying (discounting) the bill to the issuer. According to V. Anthony[2]:

> The 1960s saw a remarkable resurgence of the commercial bill . . . This was due to the adapting of the bill to new uses. The imaginative

---

[1] V. Anthony, *Banks and Markets*, Heinemann Educational Books, 1972, p. 6.
[2] Ibid.

dealers in the discount market recognized the flexibility of the instruments and institutions of the market as suppliers of credit. While the traditional bill continued to decline the finance bill, entirely an instrument of short-term credit, enjoyed a considerable growth. The finance bill could be defined as a commercial bill which involves no exchange of goods but simply a promise to pay a certain sum of money on a given date. The bills could be drawn against stocks of goods in a warehouse. They may be drawn by finance companies and accepted by merchant banks.

4. *Hire-purchase credit.* Finance houses operate by extending funds to firms in the form of hire purchase credit, to enable them to purchase plant, equipment and so on. Finance houses, like commercial banks, obtain capital by accepting deposits from customers, including other firms; they also borrow from banks and other financial institutions. Under an industrial hire-purchase arrangement, the borrowing firm pays an initial cash deposit to the seller of the equipment, to whom the finance house then makes up the difference of the rest of the selling price. The borrowing firm agrees to pay off its hire-purchase debt to the finance house over a given period and at a specified rate of interest. Although the finance houses dominate the hire purchase scene, a proportion of such finance (about one-third) is provided direct by supplier firms having the necessary legal and financial expertise.

5. *Tax reserves.* When earlier examining company accounts we saw that firms deem it prudent to set aside financial reserves to meet taxes on their profits. The precise tax liability is actually assessed and collected by the tax authorities some time after the period when the profit was earned (with the exception of the 'advance' element of corporation tax introduced in 1974). Provided then that its trading prospects are reasonably stable a firm may safely use its tax reserves as a source of short-term finance, which can be used to help run the business.

6. *Specialized export finance.* The commercial banks provide firms with specialized credit arrangements at favourable rates of interest, to help finance their exports. The credits may be extended either to the British supplier or to the foreign buyer of exports. The term of finance has, typically, been up to about six months or one year. Since the risk element in this type of business tends to be rather high, exporters obtaining the credits are required to insure themselves through a government agency known as the Export Credits Guarantee Depart-

ment. In recent years the commercial banks have, with the backing of the Department, extended their service to provide much longer term finance of up to five years or more, particularly for exports of capital goods. In 1965 outstanding export credits made available by banks under the export finance scheme amounted to about £300 millions. By 1970 this had risen to £1000 millions, covering nearly three-fifths of all export credits.

Finance for the smaller firm

Large firms enjoy a substantial financial advantage over small and medium-sized firms. For provided they can satisfy the Stock Exchange and Companies Acts conditions relating to public joint stock companies, they are able – at most times – to raise large amounts of share and debenture capital relatively cheaply on the open market. Whereas for the small or medium-sized firm – typically a partnership or private company – the costs of going public and raising capital on the open market would be prohibitive. In some countries, firms below a certain level of assets are actually forbidden to become public companies. In Britain the Stock Exchange's criteria are more flexible; generally, a proposed share capital of around £500,000 would be considered minimum entry requirements for would-be public companies.

It follows that the *quality* of smaller firm's capital structure tends to suffer from their lack of access to public funds, since this makes it difficult for them to achieve the advantage of a low gearing based on a substantial share capital. Moreover, smaller firms sometimes find it difficult to obtain any sort of genuine long-term loan finance at all, and are consequently forced into reliance on short-term credit – often from banks – which, although it may normally be renewable, might in a period of financial stringency (such as 1974) be abruptly withdrawn. In addition firms in this situation may be vulnerable to sudden and damaging increases in short-term interest rates (again, as in 1974 – see Chapter 7).

Back in the 1930s, the Macmillan Committee had found that there was a capital-raising gap affecting smaller firms, which could seriously impede their development into mature businesses operating on a large scale. One result of that investigation was the setting up, in due course, of semi-official institutions such as the ICFC and the FCI to provide medium-term finance for smaller firms.

In 1969 the Bolton Committee was set up by the government to re-examine the role of small firms in Britain's economy and to identify the problems which might threaten their development or survival. The Committee's definition of small firm varied from industry to industry; in manufacturing the criterion was less than 200 employees, in mining less than 25 employees and in the motor trade less than £100,000 turnover per year. The Bolton Committee found there were about 820,000 small firms in Britain, producing between them 18 per cent of the net output of the private sector. It was discovered that, although earning on average a better return on capital than larger firms, small firms were nevertheless steadily declining in numbers. Concerning finance, the Committee's investgation confirmed that the extreme dependence of small firms on short-term bank-credit was a serious disadvantage at times of credit squeeze.

The Committee's recommendations to help small firms included the following:

(i) Advice bureaux should be set up to give small firms better information about sources of external finance.
(ii) Corporation tax on smaller companies should be reduced, in view of their dependence on retained earnings.
(iii) Inflation accounting (see p. 89) should be adopted to help reduce the tax burden of small firms.
(iv) Companies with an annual turnover of less than £500 should be exempted from the obligation under the 1967 Companies Act to disclose their finances – this would reduce their administration and accounting work.

Additional measures to help small firms

We think that small businesses can make a special contribution because they can provide jobs faster than the big corporations – and they've always been a seedbed for new techniques and new ideas.

There is a developing policy in which the Government is going to show a continual responsiveness to the needs of small firms.

These two statements by government ministers in 1978 typify the increased role envisaged for the small-firm sector in official industrial strategy. As regards taxation, the 1977 Finance Act raised the ceiling for the reduced rate of corporation tax (42 per cent) to £40,000 and allowed marginal reliefs on profits up to £65,000; the VAT system for retailers was simplified and the registration limit raised; and small firms benefited from stock appreciation relief and rating reliefs. In 1977 a small-firms employment subsidy was introduced to provide £20 a week, for 26 weeks, for extra jobs in firms with up to 200 employees in special development areas. In the 1978 Budget the limits for VAT registration and for reduced corporation tax liability were again raised. In his speech the Chancellor referred to further proposals to help small businesses and encourage investment in them, including the availability of finance in suitable quantities and types. The 1978 tax help to small businesses was expected to amount to over £200 million a year.

Specialized sources of finance for smaller firms

Two semi-official specialist institutions were created in 1945 to help supply long-term finance to smaller firms, including many private companies. One of these institutions was the *Finance Corporation for Industry*. Its initial funds of £25 millions were obtained from the Bank of England and from a number of investment and insurance firms, and were intended to be a base for substantial additional borrowing operations. By 1970 the FCI's investments in smaller firms were approaching £400 millions, in the form, mainly, of mortgaged loan capital for periods up to 20 years. The other institution was the *Industrial and Commercial Finance Corporation*. Starting with a capital of £25 millions from the Bank of England and the commercial banks, together with large borrowing powers, the ICFC had by 1970 built up a financial stake in private industry of about £125 millions. In 1973 these two institutions were absorbed into *Finance for Industry* (see p. 105). Equity Capital for Industry (ECI) was set up in 1976, at the instigation of the Bank of England, on the basis of a £41 millions subscription by insurance companies and pension funds. The purpose of ECI is to provide equity for successful companies capitalized at £1 million to £20 millions at periods when share issues would be too expensive. ECI's funds were however so small that most of its early investments were limited to around £1 million. Among privately financed institutions designed to provide capital for the smaller firm, we may note the *Charterhouse Industrial Development Company* which was set up in 1934 by the Charterhouse Investment Trust, the Prudential Insurance Company, and Lloyds and the Midlands Banks. As we saw earlier (p. 28) the Midland Bank has more recently developed its own term-loan scheme in this field. The Small Business Capital Fund, the Gresham Trust and Moracrest

33

Investments (which is owned by a pension fund) also buy equity in, and lend to, small unquoted companies.

The sources and uses of business finance: a comment

The reader may wish to ask 'What connection, if any, is there between the various sources of a company's funds and their application within the business?' The broad answer would be that there is a connection, but that it is rather flexible. Consider the case of external long-term finance. As we have seen, this is normally associated, particularly in the case of debentures, with the acquisition of fixed assets. Nevertheless, it may be quite feasible, provided the terms in question are attractive to investors, for a company to issue securities with the object of financing current assets or even reducing current liabilities such as a bank overdraft. In the first part of 1975 there were a number of instances of companies making rights issues[1] of shares for such purposes. Conversely, a company might decide to finance fixed assets by means of short-term funds, such as a bank overdraft; generally though, this arrangement would have the disadvantage of being less certain, and perhaps more expensive, than the use of long-term capital. Turning next to internal finance, we saw in Chapter 1 that a company's depreciation funds may, at its discretion, be transformed into fixed or current assets as appropriate. Finally, there is the case of a company's reserve. In principle this constitutes long-term share capital, yet the uses to which it is put may vary from the construction of premises with an expected 50-year life, to a 3 months' currency speculation on the foreign exchange market! It can be seen therefore that whilst there are broad constraints on how a company uses its various sources of business finance, within these constraints there is a very considerable degree of flexibility.

---

[1] page 41.

BUSINESS FINANCE AND THE NEW ISSUE MARKET

Introduction
In the first two chapters of this book we looked at the part played by share capital and debenture capital as forms of business finance. In this chapter we shall be studying the mechanism whereby public companies actually obtain such finance. This is provided by the new issue market which consists of institutions in the City of London which are connected with, though not actually part of, the Stock Exchange. We shall be examining the new issue market in three stages:

1. The functions of the issuing houses.
2. Methods of issuing company securities.
3. The role of the specialist financial intermediaries, including investment trusts and unit trusts.

1. The functions of an issuing house
A company wishing to raise capital through a public issue of securities will employ the services of a specialist firm known as an *issuing house*. Some of these are well-known merchant banks, others are finance houses or even stockbroking firms. An issuing house works on a commission basis and has five main functions.

(a) *Investigating its client*
The first job of an issuing house is to find out if its client firm's prospects are sufficiently good to justify the public issue of securities. For it would not wish to endanger the savings of the investing public, or its own reputation, by promoting a badly run company which might run into difficulties. First, the issuing house will need full details of the company's past performance, in the form of audited copies of its balance sheets and income statements. It will also require:

preliminary details of the history of the business; its present size and scope; the extent of any export business; who is responsible for its running; the turnover and profits for at least ten years (if it has been in existence for that long); whether sales are going up or down; the nature, extent and value of the assets; the total and nature of the liabilities; the size and nature of any commitment to build factories or for other capital development; whether the business can be expanded; and the reason for raising new capital, offering some of the existing capital or otherwise 'going public'.[1]

The issuing house will also send its own representative to its client to make his own investigation of its management, performance and prospects. Only after its client has met all these conditions will the issuing house decide it can safely go ahead and promote the issue. If, as is likely, the company wants its securities to be dealt in on the stock market, the Stock Exchange Council will also need to carry out its own appraisal of its prospects.

It will be necessary, in accordance with the Companies Acts, for an advertisement known as a *prospectus* to appear in the press, giving investors information on the company's position. The prospectus will include: the purpose of the issue, which will probably be to finance the expansion of the company's fixed or current assets, (although it might be to repay debts, or even to finance the take-over of another firm); the nature and history of the company; the quality of its management; an accountant's summary of the profit and turnover over the last ten years, together with the present value of net assets, after allowing for all liabilities; the capital structure of the company, in respect of the relative importance of the various classes of loan and share capital; future prospects for turnover and profits; and an application form on which the public can apply for the security.

It is clear that preparing the ground for a public issue of company securities is a complicated and expensive procedure! In addition, the company concerned will have to face the further costs of allocating and underwriting the issue (see below). Consequently it would not be worthwhile for a smaller firm to seek to go public and raise capital on the open market. At the present time Stock Exchange requirements for a firm wishing to go public are that its proposed share capital should be in the region of £500,000.

---

[1] Gordon Cummings, *The Complete Guide to Investment*, Penguin Books, 1973, p. 198.

(b) *The type of security to be issued*

We have already examined, in Chapters 1 and 2, the significance of share- and debenture-finance, and their suitability for the varying circumstances of different companies. All that is necessary here, therefore, is to note that an important function of an issuing house is to use its experience to advise on the most appropriate form of security to be issued for its client company.

(c) *Pitching the terms of the issue*

Suppose it is decided that an issue of debentures would be the most appropriate method of raising finance for a particular company. (Incidentally, this sometimes suits the position of a group of directors with a majority shareholding, who do not wish to weaken their control by issuing more shares). It will now be the responsibility of the issuing house to gauge the right rate of interest to ensure that the debenture issue is successfully floated. If the interest rate offered is too low compared with that on the debentures issued by other companies of comparable standing, the investors may not fully take up the issue. On the other hand, if the issuing house decides on an interest rate which turns out to be higher than that necessary to secure the investing public's support, its client company will be loaded for the life-time of the debentures with a higher burden of interest payments than its competitors. Similar considerations apply in the case of an issue of preference shares.

In the case of ordinary shares the issuing house will be faced with the difficult task of deciding what prospective dividend is needed to float the issue.

Take the case of the company we considered on page 17. It had available for dividends an expected sum of £80,000. On the basis of a 2% dividend it should, we saw, be able to raise £4 million in shares. If its share capital was divided into, say, four million shares these would then be offered on the market at £1 each. Suppose however the issuing house had actually misjudged the mood of the market, as shown by the fact that when market dealings commenced the shares immediately settled at around £1.25, equivalent to a prospective dividend of only 1.67 per cent. Clearly, by pitching the offer (on the basis of a 2 per cent yield) at only £1 the issuing house had in fact been over-cautious, and deprived its client company of a possible £1 million of share capital.

Sometimes, though, an issuing house makes the opposite mistake: it optimistically issues the shares at what turns out to be too low a prospective dividend – that is, at an offer price which was too high to attract many investors. The share issue will then 'flop', which will be costly for the underwriter, and perhaps damaging to the client company's reputation and financial standing. The issuing house should, if it is doing its job properly, gauge the market for the shares very finely and offer them at the price which brings in the maximum amount of share capital.

During the great stock market slump of 1973–1974 (see Chapter 7) there were occasions when issuing houses badly misjudged the market, and floated share issues at an excessively high offer price, which led to them being badly *undersubscribed* by investors. More often, however, they have been criticized for being too cautious and under-pricing share issues. An investigation in 1963 by A. J. Merrett and others[1] showed that many issues of shares had taken place at an offer price well below their true market value. Many of these issues were consequently *oversubscribed* by investors. For example Penguin Books shares issued in 1961 at 60 pence were over-subscribed 150 times – though this was partly due to stagging (see p. 58) – and quickly went to 80 pence on the market. It should be noted that shares are not necessarily issued at their *nominal* or *par value*. Thus one million shares with a par value of 20 pence might be issued at a price of, say, 50 pence. In this case we would say that the share had been *issued at a premium*. (More rarely, a share may be issued below its par value – that is, *at a discount*). In principle the particular par value placed on a share should make no difference: if there are one million shares in a company, the owner of one share will receive one-millionth of the total ordinary dividend declared – regardless of its par value. What should really matter to the investor is the yield he expects to get in terms of the actual price he has paid for the share. Logically, there is no reason why a company's shares should have any par value at all. In the United States in fact a company may issue *no par shares*, its ordinary share capital simply being described as 'surplus, being divided into one million shares of no par value'. Psychologically however British investors seem to be put off by no par value shares – or, indeed, by shares issued at a big premium.

[1] A. J. Merrett, M. Howe and G. D. Newbould, *Equity Issues and the London Capital Market*, Longmans, 1967, chapter 6.

(d) *Underwriting the issue*

The Companies Acts lay down that an offer of securities, whatever the conditions, must be fully subscribed at the actual time of launching. This is intended to safeguard investors who, in the event of an issue which badly failed, might otherwise be left holding worthless securities. Issuing houses therefore arrange for issues to be *underwritten* either by themselves or by outside specialist firms which, for a commission (of up to about 3 per cent of the value of the issue) guarantee to take up any unsold securities. If the offer turns out to be fully subscribed the *underwriters* will be relieved of further responsibility. If the offer is under-subscribed however the underwriters will be required to take up the un-subscribed part of the issue. The subsequent market value of the security is then likely to be less than the issue price. So the underwriters will either have to sell the securities on the open market at a loss, or hold them in the hope that they can be sold at a better price at a later date.

(e) *Allocating the issue*

Every company prospectus contains an invitation to the public to apply for the security (usually on the basis of a minimum amount offered) together with a date for opening and closing the application. Successful applications for shares must generally be paid for in one lump sum, but there are occasions when payment may be made in two or more instalments. In the case of debentures, where the unit of issue is usually around £100 and where the size of the issue is often much greater than for shares, investors are allowed to pay on a deposit-and-instalment basis.

When an offer of securities is poorly subscribed the application lists may stay open for the full period. But if the issue proves very popular, the lists may be closed within a few minutes of the opening date. In this case investors will often be rationed – the smaller applications being perhaps accepted in full, and the larger applications scaled down appropriately. One effect of rationing is to widen the number of shareholders, which may help to ensure a ready market for the security when dealings commence on the Stock Exchange. An alternative method would be to allot the security in question by ballot.

Successful applicants for a company security receive, within a few days, *allotment letters*, which set out the amount of the security they have obtained, together with a cheque for any unsuccessful part of their application. The remainder of the applicants have their cheques returned. Open market dealings in the security on the Stock Exchange then begin about a week after the application closing date. For this purpose an investor's allotment letter needs to be exchanged for a *certificate of ownership*.

2. Methods of issuing securities

There are five main methods of issuing company securities:

(a) One method, which we have in fact just been examining above, is called a public issue *by prospectus*. As we saw, in this method the issuing house floats the securities to the general public at a given price.

(b) Another method is an *offer for sale*. This is similar to a public issue, the main difference being that the entire block of securities is first bought outright at a specified price by the issuing house itself, which then disposes of them to investors at a rather higher price. This method, which is favoured by the Stock Exchange Council, has in fact now become the most common method of issuing company securities.

(c) *Placing an issue* is mainly used when the issue is small, or likely to lack public interest. In this method the issuing house sells or *places* securities which it has previously purchased or subscribed for, to its own private clients, including stock brokers, investment trusts and insurance companies. A placing tends to be cheaper than the first two methods we considered, because the allotment procedure is more straightforward and the prospectus information required less detailed.

A factor which inhibited placings was the Stock Exchange's *pre-emption rule*, which required listed companies to offer existing shareholders first claim to newly issued shares, and so effectively limited access to the placing market by most big companies. The dropping of this rule, in 1975, thus widened the market for placings.

(d) A more recent (and controversial) method of issuing securities – mainly ordinary shares – is an *issue by tender*. We saw above that one drawback of an issue by conventional methods is that the security may be issued at a lower price than the market was in fact prepared to pay. An issue by tender attempts to overcome this by inviting bids from investors, based on a minimum offer price. Here is an example of how the method works. Suppose an issuing house offers on behalf of its client company one million shares at a price of not less than

60 pence and that the tenders received from investors at various prices are as follows:

Table 3.1

Price	Shares applied for	Number of applicants
90	30,000	10
$87\frac{1}{2}$	60,000	10
85	70,000	15
$82\frac{1}{2}$	90,000	35
80	80,000	30
$77\frac{1}{2}$	90,000	40
75	150,000	60
$72\frac{1}{2}$	180,000	90
70	250,000	120
$67\frac{1}{2}$	200,000	250
65	150,000	140
$62\frac{1}{2}$	100,000	80
60	30,000	20
Total	1,480,000	900

It can be seen that altogether 900 applications were received for a total of 1,480,000 shares: the issue was thus subscribed about one-and-a-half times.

The issuing house might now if it wished make the entire allotment at a price of 70 pence, in which case all 410 applications at or above this price would be satisfied in full. It might however prefer to increase the number of shareholders, so as to help broaden the potential market in the shares. It would then select a rather lower *striking price*, such as $67\frac{1}{2}$ pence, in which case the 660 successful applicants would, as a group, be allotted fewer shares than they actually tendered for. It should be noted that all applicants would receive their shares at the common striking price of $67\frac{1}{2}$ pence irrespective of their actual tender price. The final outcome would then be that the issuing company received £675,000. This compares with the £600,000 it would have obtained by a conventional issue based on an offer price of, say, 60 pence per share.

In spite of its obvious advantages, the issue-by-tender method has attracted criticism and remained relatively uncommon. One criticism has been that tenders by the general investing public are less likely to result in a realistic issue price than a conventional issue arranged by experts. The evidence however suggests the opposite – namely, that striking prices for issues by tender have generally been quite near the true market prices of the security concerned. Another criticism has been that the tender method creates relatively little public interest, and so may lead to an unnecessary high allotment price – particularly if stag investors are frightened off (see p. 55).

(e) A *rights issue* of shares is unlike the other methods so far described, in that it is made directly to a company's existing shareholders and therefore by-passes the main mechanism of the new issue market. From a company viewpoint, a rights issue has the advantage that no prospectus is needed, and the only advertising costs are for the letters of rights sent to its existing shareholders.

Here is an example of how a rights issue works. Suppose a company's share capital consists of two million shares of £1 par value, having a current market price of £2. If it wished to raise £500,000 of new capital, it would then make its shareholders a rights issue of 500,000 £1 shares. The offer would take the form of a *letter of entitlement* giving each shareholder the right to apply for one new £1 share at par, for every four shares at present held. In this situation a shareholder would be faced with two main courses of action. The first would be to take up the full amount of his entitlement. In the case of a shareholder having 40,000 shares, this would mean purchasing 10,000 further shares at a total cost of £10,000. Now on the face of it this would seem to be the best thing to do. For the investor is apparently getting a real bargain, paying £10,000 par value for shares which are worth, at £2 each on the stock market, £20,000, thus making a 'gain' of £10,000! However there is a catch: the rights issue, by increasing the supply of the company's shares would reduce their market price! The new market price would in fact be determined as follows:

Table 3.2

Original market value of company	£4,000,000
Funds raised by rights issue	£500,000
New market value of company	£4,500,000
New number of shares	2,500,000
New market price per share	£1·80

Therefore the investor's net position would actually be as follows:

Table 3.3

Number of shares held	Original value	New value	Change
40,000	£80,000	£72,000	−£8,000
10,000	£10,000 (par)	£18,000	+£8,000
50,000	£90,000	£90,000	nil

We see that the gain which the shareholder makes on the rights shares is precisely offset by the fall in the market value of his existing holding: in effect he has merely increased his shareholding, at market value, by £10,000 – and paid precisely £10,000 to do so! However if he considers his existing shares a good investment he will presumably be satisfied at the opportunity, through the rights issue, of increasing it.

The second situation arises when a shareholder does not wish to take advantage of a rights issue. One possibility would be for him to do absolutely nothing, and simply allow his rights to lapse. This however would be a mistake, for as we have just seen, the market price of his existing shares will in any case fall, which would then leave him worse off than before. The correct course therefore could be for him to *sell* his letter of entitlement to the new shares to another investor. Since the new market price of the shares is likely to be around 180 pence, an investor wishing to purchase the rights should be willing to pay up to 80 pence entitlement per new share (this would in fact normally be expressed as 40 pence per old share). The shareholder selling the rights would then receive 10,000 × 80 pence = £8,000. Taking into account the equivalent fall in the market value of the original 40,000 shares which he continues to hold, he will be left, overall, with neither a loss nor a gain. However his decision will have somewhat reduced the market value of his shareholding in the company. If he wished exactly to maintain this, he would sell an appropriate part only of his rights entitlement, and use the proceeds to take up the remainder of his rights.

Share issues which reorganize a company's capital
In addition to the five methods examined above, there are two further methods of issuing shares, namely an *issue by introduction* and a *scrip issue*. What these have in common is the fact that, unlike the other methods, they do not increase the amount of a company's capital, they are merely designed to reorganize its form.

43

(a) An introduction is designed to allow a company whose shares are already quite widely held, to increase their marketability by obtaining a quotation for stock exchange dealings. As in the case of an issue by placing, which it resembles, a prospectus will need to be published and there will also have to be a satisfactory vetting by the Quotation Department of the Stock Exchange. A common motive for seeking an introduction is that the firm in question – often a private company – wishes to prepare the way for future expansion, via new public share issues, by increasing public interest and the potential market in its shares. Another motive may be that some of the larger shareholders in a company wish to sell their holdings – for example, to provide for the payment of estate duty. As in the case of a placing, and for similar reasons, the cost of an issue by introduction tends to be relatively low. Although there is no marketing in the normal sense, jobbers are given options on the shares at a stated price, so as to facilitate the growth of an active market.

(b) The background to a scrip issue is often one in which a company has for some years been steadily expanding out of its own profits and finds that the share capital originally subscribed by its shareholders has become a quite small part of the funds which it now employs. Consequently, the profits being earned, and dividends paid, when expressed on the basis of a very limited share capital, are likely to be very high, as indeed will be the market price of each share. A disadvantage of this situation is that an apparently high rate of dividend may expose the company to the charge of profiteering and involve it in undesirable publicity. Secondly, a high market price may deter the investing public from buying the company's shares – which is quite illogical for, other things being equal, the earnings and dividend prospects of ten £1 shares in a given company are exactly the same as for one £10 share!

In order to overcome these difficulties a company may decide to *capitalize* its reserves by issuing 'free' scrip shares on a pro-rata basis to its shareholders. For example, if it had a share capital of £1 millions, and a retained reserve of £2·5 millions (giving it a net equity of £3·5 millions) it might decide to make a two-for-one (200 per cent) scrip issue. This would involve issuing each shareholder with two free shares for every one share previously held. The company's share capital would then be increased from £1 million to £3 millions, leaving only £0·5 million in reserve form. Clearly, its net equity of £3·5 millions would not in any way have changed as a result of the scrip issue, nor would the dividend prospects per shareholder. So, if the old dividend rate per share was, say, 24 per cent, the new rate would now be 8 per cent. There would also be a corresponding decline in the market value of the shares: if the price of the shares before the scrip issue was 180 pence, the new price would settle around 60 pence (the supply of the shares having trebled). Sometimes, though, investors may interpret the reorganization of a company's capital as a sign of more dynamic management and better future dividends. The effect may then be to increase the demand for, and the market price of, its shares.

Another point to note is that a scrip issue is sometimes made in the form of *non-voting shares*, the aim being to retain the controlling interest of the company in the hands of existing equity holders. In recent years opposition to non-voting shares has grown, partly on account of the scope which they give for take-over bids. Many of the big institutional investors, such as insurance companies, pension funds and investment trusts, have expressed their disapproval by refusing to purchase non-voting shares; more recently the Stock Exchange Council itself has criticized the practice of issuing them.

One final point: it is possible for a company to make a combined *scrip-plus-rights issue*, in which it not only increases its existing nominal equity, but also at the same time raises fresh capital. Readers who are interested in the mechanics of such an operation should consult one of the more specialized texts listed in the bibliography at the end of this book.

(3) Specialist financial intermediaries

Hitherto in this book we have, both in the context of new issues and of stock market dealings, usually spoken for simplicity of the investing public. It is now necessary to qualify this. Whilst it is true that private individuals represent a considerable element in both markets, a dominant part has over the years come to be played by the *institutional investors*. We saw an instance of this earlier in connection with the placing of an issue, where it is the institutions which mainly take up the security in question. There are four main types of institutional investor:

(a) *The insurance companies*. There are several hundred of these in Britain. One part of their activity (the general business) consists in providing persons and firms with insurance against various types of risk. Their other main activity is the life business, whereby individuals are in effect enabled to save, by making to an insurance company regular payments (premiums) which provide assurance benefits against the death of the policy holder. The insurance companies in their turn invest their funds in various directions, including company securities.

(b) *Pension funds.* Many people pay a specified proportion of their earnings – or have it paid for them by their employers – into a *pension fund,* from which on retirement they will collect a pension. Formerly, the main part of the pension funds was, for safety, invested in government securities; in recent years however an increasing proportion has been going into company securities – until the 1974 share crash underlined some of the dangers.

(c) *Unit trusts.* A unit trust is a method of pooling the resources of many small investors, so that their savings can be safely spread over a range of securities. A unit trust must have a paid-up capital of over £500,000 and its funds are invested by professional managers, subject to the role of a *trustee* – usually a bank or insurance company – who ensures that the Board of Trade's legal requirements concerning trusts are observed (for example, that the securities selected are in types of industries specified in the trust, and that the maximum amount which may be invested in any one company's security is not exceeded).

An investor in a unit trust receives his entitlement to a share of the trust's income on the basis of the number of *units* which he has purchased in it. If the investor decides to withdraw his savings from the trust, the managers will re-purchase his units on request. Naturally the price of units will reflect the underlying market value of the securities held by the trust. If these are doing well, the market value of the trust's units will increase; if, on the other hand (as in the 1973–1974 slump in security prices) the value of the unit trust's investment falls, so too, will the price of its units. An attractive feature of the units is that they are very easy to buy: no broker is needed, one merely fills in and posts a coupon. Incidentally, unit trusts are allowed to advertise their services.

(d) *Investment trusts.* The function of an investment trust is in many ways similar to that of a unit trust: it pools and spreads the savings of many small investors. However there are two important differences between an investment trust and a unit trust. First (and in spite of its name) an investment trust is not in fact a trust at all! It is actually a *company*, the main assets of which consist of the securities of other companies. Under the terms of the 1965 Finance Act, investment trusts are required to pay out 85 per cent of their investment income, the remainder being allowed to be retained for future operations. Many of the investment trusts are associated with, and partly financed by, well-known merchant banks. The investing public can invest in an investment trust by buying its shares – just as they would with any other joint stock company.

The second difference is that, unlike a unit trust, an investment trust is free to raise loan capital and thus get the benefits of a reduced gearing (see p. 23) for its shareholders. It must be remembered though that in the event of a downturn in security prices, and hence the value of an investment trust's assets and income, this reduced gearing could prove a serious disadvantage for its shareholders – as the experience of the 1974 financial crash was to show (see Chapter 7).

Table 3.4   Asset portfolios of institutional investors, end–1976

Market value (£ millions)

	Unit trusts	Investment trusts	Insurance companies	Pension funds
Net current assets	351	322	1,922	983
Central and local Government securities	35	176	6,742	3,643
Company securities				
Debentures	23	194	1,957 ⎫	
Preference	45	74	266 ⎬	9,077
Ordinary	2,168	5,170	8,191 ⎭	
Unit trusts	—	—	516	53
Loans and mortgages	—	—	3,157	379
Land and property	—	—	5,584	2,349
Other	—	132	1,614	183
Total	2,622	6,068	29,949	16,627

Source: *Financial Statistics*, H M S O.

4
THE WORKINGS OF THE STOCK EXCHANGE

Jobbers and brokers

We saw in Chapter 1 that the Stock Exchange, which constitutes a secondary market for securities, backs up the working of the new issue market, on which companies raise new capital via shares and debentures. The operation of the Stock Exchange revolves around the activities of two types of dealers: brokers and jobbers. The brokers earn their living on a commission basis, by acting as agents for investors wishing to buy or sell securities on the Stock Exchange. The jobbers on the other hand are the wholesalers of the Stock Exchange: they hold, or have available on their own behalf, securities which they buy from, and sell to, the brokers acting for the investing public. Many jobbers are quite small firms – partnerships or private companies – operating partly with their own capital and partly on borrowed funds.

Suppose an investor decides to buy 500 of the 25 pence (par) ordinary shares in the firm of XYZ Ltd. He will telephone the order to his broker, who will then go (or send his clerk) to the part of the Stock Exchange floor where the jobbers who deal in XYZ shares are located. The broker, taking care not to reveal whether he is buying or selling for his client will ask one of the jobbers, 'What are XYZ?' The jobber may reply, '$82\frac{1}{2}$–85'. This means that he would be prepared to buy the shares at $82\frac{1}{2}$ pence each, or sell them at 85 pence. The difference between these two prices is known as the jobber's turn (it is often, mistakenly, page 50, believed to constitute a jobber's income). The next jobber whom our broker asks may reply '83–86': that is, he would be prepared to buy XYZ shares at 83 pence or sell them at 86 pence. The list of quotations which the broker finally gets, then, might look like this:

Table 4.1	Buy	Sell
Jobber A	$82\frac{1}{2}$	85
Jobber B	83	86
Jobber C		$85\frac{1}{2}$
Jobber D	84	
Jobber E	$83\frac{1}{2}$	$85\frac{1}{2}$

It will be noted that jobber C, although willing to supply XYZ shares, is not at present prepared to buy any, while jobber D is prepared to buy XYZ shares but not at present to sell them. (In fact, there are times when, contrary to what is often believed, a jobber may call off dealing altogether in a particular security – particularly at times of great uncertainty on the market.)

The broker will now decide to deal with the cheapest of the four supplying jobbers, namely A, and perhaps bargain some more, so beating him down to, say, $84\frac{1}{2}$ pence. (If the broker had been selling for his client he would probably have done business with jobber D.) The jobber and the broker will now complete the deal by making an entry in their note books. When all the necessary paper work has later been completed, the broker's client will in due course receive his certificate of ownership for 500 XYZ shares. It should be noted that Stock Exchange bargains are struck for not in cash, but for future settlement (see p. 52). This not only saves time but also allows convenient settlement between the first seller and final buyer of a security, after adjustment for any intervening deals which may have taken place.

The jobber as a principal

Jobber A may in fact already have on his books a substantial number of XYZ shares, which he has previously obtained from brokers selling on behalf of clients. In this case he can go ahead and deliver the order for the 500 XYZ shares. It may happen, though, that he holds no XYZ shares at all at present. He must then buy some from a broker and this will need to be done within the standard period of dealing on the Stock Exchange, which are called *accounts*, most of which last for two weeks. So, the next time a broker comes along and asks about XYZ shares, jobber A, hoping that he is a potential seller, may make his offer price more attractive by quoting, say, $83\frac{1}{2}$–$85\frac{1}{2}$. If he succeeds in obtaining the XYZ shares at $83\frac{1}{2}$, he will then have made a gross profit of 1 penny per share ($84\frac{1}{2}$–$83\frac{1}{2}$) on the combined transaction. If however, very few XYZ shares are coming on to the market, he might have to quote, say, 89–91 to obtain XYZ shares. In this event he would have made a loss on the combined deal of $4\frac{1}{2}$ pence (89–$84\frac{1}{2}$ pence) per share – in total, £22.50.

It is clear then that unless a jobber happens to buy and sell a share simultaneously, the turn which he quotes for a security at any particular time in no way measures the profit he is making. Jobbers (when successful) make their living in fact mainly by anticipating future movements in security prices: selling for future delivery securities whose market price they consider will fall, and buying those whose price is likely to rise. Around 1974 many jobbers ran into difficulties in this respect, on account of rapidly falling share prices, which made it very hard to predict future prices. (Another difficulty at that time was that, in a nervous market, dealings in securities declined considerably, which further reduced the earnings of the jobbers, and brokers.)

Jobbers and market forces
When a jobber is short of a particular security, he will increase his offer price in order to attract orders from brokers. Conversely, a jobber who is in danger of being overloaded with a particular security will reduce his bid price, so as to deter brokers who may be selling it and encourage brokers buying it. A jobber can also, by varying the size of his turn, regulate the amount of business he wishes to do in a particular security. If he widens his turn, he will deter both buying and selling in a particular security; if he narrows his turn, he will encourage both buying and selling – though, other things being equal, his profits will tend to fall if his turn becomes too narrow. The successful jobber is one who correctly anticipates the market forces of supply and demand and hence the likely future prices of securities in which he deals.

It would be quite incorrect to imagine that jobbers (or brokers, for that matter) *determine* security prices. In fact a jobber who, by trying to do so, went against the broad market trend, would quickly be forced out of business. Early in 1975 when a sensational share boom set in on the London stock market,[1] many jobbers were in fact caught facing the wrong direction, and had to pay heavily to deliver shares whose price they had wrongly expected to fall. Moreover, the successful jobber by buying cheap (when a security's price is low) and selling dear (when its price is high) not only makes a living for himself; he also helps to smooth out the trend of security prices. It is of course implicit in the above discussion that the network of stock market dealings is sufficiently competitive to allow a free expression of market forces. Whether this assumption is fully justified will be examined in Chapter 6 (see p. 74).

---

[1] See p. 107.

Stockbrokers as sources of advice and information

An important supplementary service offered by stockbrokers is to give *advice and information* to their clients. A broker should be able to help work out for his client the particular investment policy which meets his circumstances. For a person wishing to save for retirement this might be aimed (provided there is not rapid inflation) at a relatively safe income from fixed interest securities such as debentures or government stock; for a client wanting growth of income, a portfolio of ordinary shares might be recommended; for a customer wanting quick capital gains an outright speculative policy might be suggested. The stockbroker will base his advice on his own experience and on what he knows from his personal contacts in the Stock Exchange and other financial areas. Some of the larger stockbroking firms have their own research departments, which send clients regular reports on the general market outlook, together with the prospects for particular securities. In addition most brokers circulate once a year to each client the current market value of his or her holding (portfolio) of securities.

Many investors on their side take advantage of independent sources of market information, such as the financial analysis in the pages of the *Financial Times, The Investors Chronicle, Moodies Services*, and so on. Ideally, an investor should be in a position not only to seek advice from his broker but also (within limits) to discuss and qualify it. Whatever the outcome, responsibility for the actual decision will of course always rest with the investor himself. Some investors obtain advice from their banks, which in turn employ the services of their own regular stockbrokers. However it is questionable whether this is as effective as a direct and immediate contact between investor and broker. Finally, there are those investors who deal through unit trusts and investment trusts (see p. 46); here the investor is relying on the expertise of the trust's professional managers, and their brokers.

Speculation on the Stock Exchange: bulls and bears

One category of business on the Stock Exchange is accounted for by the long-term investor in company securities, seeking a steady income in the case of debentures, or a growth of income and capital in the case of shares. The Stock Exchange is however a scene of activity for a very different class of investors. We are referring here to those buying and selling securities (generally shares) in order to make quick profits over periods of time which may be as little as a few days, or even hours. There are two main categories of speculators, the *bulls* and the *bears*. It should be stressed that there is nothing special about bulls and bears – they are merely investors (amateur or professional, as the case may be) who are aiming at short-term capital gains, rather than longer-term income and growth. Bulls are speculators who are optimistic about the prospects for a given share, and, believing that its market price is likely to rise, hope to make a profit (technically, a *capital gain*) by buying it cheaply now and re-selling it at a higher price later on. Bears on the other hand are pessimists, who believe that a particular share's prospects are relatively poor and that its market price is thus likely to fall. They hope therefore to make a gain by selling the security at a high price now and buying it back cheaply later on when its price has fallen.

Speculation is significantly affected by the fact that dealings on the Stock Exchange take place within a series of periods – normally a fortnight – known as accounts. All deals are settled on a day known as *account day* or *settlement day*, which is the second Tuesday after the close of an account. The existence of the account makes it possible for bulls and bears to undertake speculative operations without the need to put up any funds, provided they cover their position by the end of the account. A bull buying shares near the start of an account would, if all went well, sell them at a higher price by the end of the account and receive a cheque for his net gain from his broker on the following settlement day. If however the share price fell the bull would be required to make a payment of loss to his stockbroker at this time. The same would apply, *mutatis mutandis*, to bears operating within the account. It can be seen that the speculative risks inherent in this situation are very large, since there is in principle no direct limit on the amount invested, or the losses of the unsuccessful speculator. In practice, however, the broker in question would be likely to become concerned about his own professional liability, if he thought that his client's speculations exceeded his resources.

It may happen that the effects of the operations of the bulls and bears in a particular share are evenly matched. In this case the net impact on the market price will be nil. Suppose however speculation becomes one-sided – for example, the bull activity in a particular share outweighs that of the bears, reflecting on balance a view that the share's earnings and dividends prospects are actually better than rated by the market. The result will be that the market price of the share will tend to rise. If the increased earnings and dividends which the bulls have been expecting are in fact later announced, the general increase in demand for the share by long-term investors will enable the bulls to sell off their holdings and take their gains. Hence the effect of the speculation will have been to moderate the amount of fluctuation in the price of the share in question. For if there had been no bull buying, the share's price would have changed little in the early stages, and then risen suddenly and sharply when the company in question announced the higher dividend. The point also applies in the other direction: bear activity will tend to depress a share's market price steadily in stages, in anticipation of bad earnings and dividend results. If there were no early selling by the bears, the share's price would change little to begin with, but would later experience a sudden and unsettling fall. Enough has been said, then, to indicate that the stock market is not necessarily harmed by, and may even benefit from, the speculative activities of bulls and bears.

The question may be asked however: what happens when a whole group of speculators, having perhaps a dominant influence on the market guess wrongly? Could they, by their actions, destabilize share prices and damage the workings of the Stock Exchange? We shall examine this important question next.

Perverse speculation

We have seen that the underlying factor in investing in a share is the expectation of receiving dividends and capital gains out of the profits of the company in question. In the end, therefore, whatever investors may originally have thought, 'the truth will out'. In other words (mixing our metaphors), the proof of the pudding is in the eating – if a share continues to pay good dividends, it is a 'good' share. The snag however is that in the time period when the market's longer-term expectations are being tested, the buying and selling decisions of speculators may, if incorrect, push the market price of the share in question to what turns out to be a very false level. Then, as the true company performance comes to be revealed, speculators will start to buy or sell the share (as the case may be) *en masse*. In this way repeated and unsettling disturbances in share prices could take place. In the words of Maynard Keynes[1]

---

[1] J. M. Keynes, *The General Theory of Employment Interest and Money*, Macmillan, 1936, p. 156.

... Professional investment may be likened to those newspaper competitions in which the competitors have to pick out the six prettiest faces from a hundred photographs, the prize being awarded to the competitor whose choice most nearly corresponds to the average preference of the competitors as a whole; so that each competitor has to pick, not those faces which he himself finds prettiest, but those which he thinks likeliest to catch the fancy of the other competitors all of whom are looking at the problem from the same point of view. It is not a case of choosing those which, to the best of one's judgement, are really the prettiest nor even those which average opinion genuinely think the prettiest. We have reached the third degree where we devote our intelligences to anticipating what average opinion expects the average opinion to be.

Thus on this interpretation of market behaviour while the broad trend of share prices might reflect the underlying profit and dividend performance of a company, erratic short-run fluctuations around it could occur, as the mood of speculators shifted from one extreme to another.

The evidence, such as it is, suggests there is some truth in this. That is to say, while the market yield of a share is often a reasonable guide on the prospects of the company in question, there is sometimes a considerable element of fashion, so that some shares retain, in the eyes of investors, a glamour no longer justified by results, while shares in unfashionable companies remain depressed some time after their fortunes have started to improve.

Another factor which needs to be considered is the effect on share prices, and yields, of a general speculative mood in the stock market as a whole. This is discussed in Chapter 7.

Speculative options

A speculator who misjudges the market in a particular share exposes himself to the risk of a large loss. For example, a bear who undertook to deliver a thousand shares (which he had not at present got), at say 30 pence, might find himself later having to complete the deal by purchasing the shares at, say, 50 pence, rather than 20 pence as he expected. He would thus make a loss of £200 on the operation. Similarly, a bull might buy shares expecting their price to rise, but find he could only re-sell them at a much reduced price, involving him in a large loss. It is possible for a speculator to limit such losses by purchasing an *option*, in the form of a right to buy or sell a share at a specified price and within a stated period – usually three months. Once during each account (generally on the first Thursday) there is a *declaration day*, when option rights can be exercised. Most options are handled by a small number of specialist jobbers, under licence from the Stock Exchange Council.

This is how options work. Suppose a bull judges that a share currently standing on the market at 100 pence is likely soon to go to around 130 pence. If he has a capital of £1,000 the potential profit to be gained from dealing in one thousand shares would be £300.[1] If he instead purchases a *call option* from a broker, costing perhaps 5 pence a share (to cover jobbing expenses) he will be able to use his £1,000 of capital to take out an option on 20,000 shares. If the shares rise as expected to 130 pence he will on re-selling them make a profit of £5,000 – from which must be subtracted broking fees and capital gains tax[2]. Suppose however he has guessed wrongly, and the shares in question fall to say 50 pence. If he then delivered the 20,000 shares at this price he would be exposed to a very large loss indeed. So it would now be better for him to abandon his option, and limit his loss to the £1,000 which he paid for it. If the shares increased in value, but by less than the cost of the option, he would make a loss equivalent to the difference between the two amounts. In practice, taking all dealing expenses, including brokerage, into consideration, the price of a share generally needs to rise by about 10 to 15 per cent before an over-all profit can be made on a call option.

A bear speculator, betting on a downward movement in the price of a share, can protect himself against an unexpected rise in its price, by purchasing a *put option* which gives him the right to sell the shares in question within three months at the stated striking price. The reader will be able to construct a simple example illustrating the mechanism of a put option.

Finally, there is the type of situation in which a company's performance is subject to factors which might carry its earnings, and thus its share price, very sharply up or down – for example, a company about to announce the results of expensive drilling operations for a key stragetic mineral. A speculator would like to be in a position to carry out either a bull transaction or a bear transaction, depending on whether the share price in fact rises or falls. One way of doing

---

[1] Less expenses, see Appendix F.
[2] Page 115.

this, and at the same time limiting the risk involved, would be by taking out a combined *call and put* option allowing him either to buy or to sell the share in question at a stated striking price. If the company's shares rose, he would discard the put option, and sell the shares at a profit. If they fell, he would discard the call option, and deliver the shares.

Traded options

1978 saw the introduction of traded options on the London and Amsterdam stock exchanges, following their introduction five years earlier in Chicago. The essential difference between conventional and traded options is that the latter are marketable. Firstly, whereas a conventional option is in principle unique in terms of the price, number of shares and time span, in the case of a traded option these characteristics are standardized. Secondly, the buyer and seller of a traded option have a contract with a clearing corporation which deals in options. The parties to the option can, therefore, act independently of each other and a secondary market in options becomes possible. The market price at which the traded option changes hands is known as the *premium*. The seller ('writer') of the option retains the money premium which may be viewed as income or as a hedge against a fall in the price of the underlying security. The buyer hopes either to purchase an option when the premium is low and re-sell later at a higher price; or to exercise the option if the price of the underlying security has moved in his favour. The buyer can take his profit (or loss) on the premium at any time. The writer can buy back his option if it is unexpired and has not been exercised and will hope to make a profit on the difference between the premiums at which he sold and bought in. If an option is exercised against a writer he is committed to deliver the security in question. In general, options with a long time-span and an underlying security which is prone to market fluctuations will, through the effects of supply and demand, carry a higher premium. As with conventional options, traded options can be taken out for the 'call' or the 'put' – giving the buyer a future right to sell or to purchase a security at a given price.

Both London and Amsterdam initially offered only 'call' facilities in traded options. In London traded options were offered for ten 'blue chip' shares with a choice of three-, six- or nine-month time spans. To the extent that trade options seem to satisfy a speculative need they might be called useful. Unfortunately they also offer scope for 'manipulative and deceptive practices', as the Securities and Exchange Commission found in 1977 in the United States where one expert called the abuses 'frightening'.

There are considered to be four requirements for an effective traded options market.[1] Firstly, education for users of the new market. While the Chicago market provides clear and frank written guidance for investors, the London exchange has been criticized for providing vague and unhelpful information. Secondly, a fair market is needed which is free from conflicting interests for dealers. The problem here is that options dealing in London were to take place on the very same floor (but not pitches) as trade in the underlying securities – a situation likely to place considerable pressure on the integrity of dealers, in spite of the options dealing code which had been set up. Thirdly, there is a requirement for an adequate financial safety net for dealings: a condition which London meets. Fourthly, there is a need for effective policing to prevent abuses; we shall later examine doubts about the effectiveness of the London stock exchange's self-surveillance arrangements (see p. 77).

It is not possible within the scope of this book to do more than offer a brief outline of traded options. For a more refined treatment, the reader is advised to refer to advanced texts, such as the authoritative article in *The Economist*[2] on which this short description has been mainly based.

Carry-over business

A bull speculating within the account may decide that although the price of some shares which he has purchased has fallen, it is nevertheless likely soon to rise substantially. He may then arrange with his broker to *carry over* his bull deal, and delay paying for the shares which he bought, until the end of the next account. If the price of the share does in fact rise sufficiently, the bull will then collect a profit cheque from his broker in the normal way on the next settlement day. Naturally, a speculator will expect to pay for the privilege of this carry-over facility (which is known as *contango*); this will take the form of an interest charge to his broker, on the speculative credit which he has obtained from him. Similarly it is possible for a bear to postpone, at a cost, delivery of shares from

---

[1] *The Economist*, 25 May, 1978, page 101.
[2] Ibid.

one account to the next. Theoretically, a speculator might arrange successive carry-over transactions spanning several accounts. The total cost of doing this would however be considerable; and so the movement in share prices needed to give an over-all profit would be correspondingly increased. The function of the brokers in regard to carry-over transactions is in effect to marry the opposing deals of the bulls and bears. When this is not fully possible some unlucky bulls or bears are sometimes thrown out and have to find other arrangements to settle their bargains.

Stagging

We saw above (p. 37) that it may be difficult for an issue house using conventional issuing methods to gauge the right price at which to offer a new issue of company shares. Often, issuing houses have tended to play for safety, by pitching the issue price of the share on the low side, and thus offering an unnecessarily attractive prospective dividend rate. When this happens an issue may be heavily over-subscribed by the investors, so that when Stock Exchange dealings start the market price of the share rises substantially. *Stags* are speculators who purchase such shares on the new issue market, in the hope of quickly re-selling them at a profit once market dealings open. Thus, whereas bulls and bears operate within the Stock Exchange market, stags straddle the new issue market and the Stock Exchange. Also, in contrast to speculation within the Stock Exchange, all stags are optimists.

The judgement of the professional stags – those who deal on a big scale, and make a living from it – may be based on an expert analysis of the past balance sheets and income statements of the company in question; the quality of its management; its financial outlook; and various other factors affecting the company's likely performance (see Chapter 2). Even so, it is quite possible for a stag to guess wrongly, and over-estimate the likely public demand for a new share. In this case, the shares which he has recently purchased may fall heavily when stock market dealings begin. He will then either have to sell them at a direct loss, or be prepared to hold them in the hope that their price later improves – in which case the (opportunity) cost of his mistake will be the alternative speculative gains which he is now sacrificing by tying up his money in one security.

There have been many occasions when the professional stags have been joined by large numbers of amateur stags sensing the possibilities of quick capital gains. An example of mass-stagging was provided by an ordinary-share issue in 1974 by the food firm of Sains-bury. When the terms of the issue were announced it became clear that widespread public interest would almost certainly lead to a heavy over-subscription. Some speculators even went to the point of writing out cheques for large amounts which they did not even have, knowing – or hoping – that their speculative proceeds would cover them. In the event the shares did in fact go to a premium on the market. And so (from the point of view of stags who were lucky enough to be allotted shares), a good time was had by all. It was on account of abuses of this kind that some issuing houses began to insist on cash subscription for new issues, together with a limit on individual subscriptions. Even so, some eager stags have found a way round this limitation by subscribing to new share issues through friends and relatives.

It is sometimes held that stagging operations, when based on a sound appraisal of a company's prospects, are beneficial to the operation of the new issue market, since they make it easier to float off an issue of company securities. In effect, it is argued, the stags can be regarded as providing temporary short-term finance to support an issue until sufficient longer-term finance becomes avail-able via the stock market from conventional investors. Against this must be set the fact that heavy over-subscription by stags adds very greatly to the expenses of issuing houses faced with extremely large numbers of applications: as, for example, in the case of an issue of shares by Headquarter and General Supply Limited in 1963, which was over-subscribed 177 times.

It is worth noting that one aim of the short-term capital gains tax which was introduced in 1962 (see p. 120), was to reduce the hitherto tax-free profits made by stags (and other speculators). In the event stagging activity did not decline: speculators presumably took the view that half a loaf was better than none. However, the use of the tender method of issuing shares (p. 40), by enabling issuing houses to pitch the issue price of a security much nearer to their true market value, has been quite effective in cutting the ground away from the stags.

5

THE SIGNIFICANCE OF THE STOCK EXCHANGE

The Stock Exchange and the allocation of investment resources
We saw earlier that the relative prices and yields of different companies' securities help to shape the way in which they are able to
raise capital on the open market. More theoretically, it can be
stated that:

> In its ideal form, an active stock market, operating in an economy
> where there is a wide dispersal of share ownership, provides the
> mechanism whereby the money savings of individuals and other
> economic units are pooled together and then allocated to those pro-
> ducing units where they are expected to find their most profitable use.
> If private profitability is assumed to be an indicator of 'efficiency' in
> the normal calculus of a capitalist economy, a perfect stock market
> (with equilibrium prices based on an accurate forecasting of future
> profits) would bring about an efficient allocation of the available
> savings.[1]

Moreover:

> The pricing of securities is the principal device by which the stock
> market performs its allocative functions. By assigning higher prices to
> the securities of the firm with higher prospective earnings per unit of
> resources, and relatively lower prices to those of firms with low pros-
> pective profitability, the market can ensure that the more 'efficient'
> firms have cheaper access to investment funds and are therefore able
> to make greater use of them.[2]

A good example was provided by the movement of British Leyland Motor Company shares in 1974. The general decline in the
demand for motor cars, following from higher petrol prices, coupled
with the BLMC management's inability to overcome a number of
internal problems, eventually pushed that company near to insolvency. Well before the point was reached, however, the market price

---

[1] Ajit Singh, *Take-overs, their Relevance to the Stock Market and the
Theory of the Firm*, Cambridge University Press, 1970, p. 2.
[2] Ibid.

of BLMC shares had started falling remorselessly, as investment analysis increasingly revealed the grim financial outlook for BLMC. How reliable is the investment allocator? We shall be examining this question in Chapter 6 (p. 82).

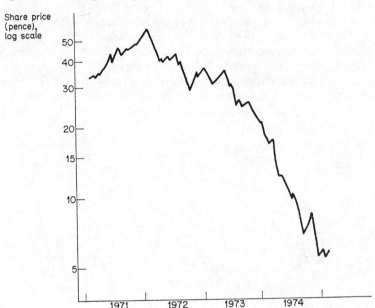

Fig. 5.1. The decline in British Leyland shares 1971–1974.

Not only does the stock market system of security pricing help to allocate investment resources between the companies (and industries) competing for their use; it also acts as a 'macro-barometer' for the investment outlook of the economy as a whole, by highlighting the *general* prospects for the broad range of private business activity. During boom periods when demand is high and companies are working at a high level of output, business profits and dividends per share tend to increase, and this becomes reflected in rising security prices on the stock market. If the further outlook for new investment opportunities also seems good the general level of share prices may be driven extremely high, reflecting the fact that investors are prepared to accept a very low current market yield in the expectation that they will eventually be rewarded with much higher dividends in the future out of the growing profits of companies. For example, during the 1972 stock market boom investors were prepared to hold shares in a number of the most promising companies at market yields of less than one per cent! As a result it became possible for these companies to raise capital very cheaply indeed. When a business downturn seems likely, however, and investors are pessimistic about the outlook for further profits and reluctant to hold company securities, falling share prices and rising market yields make it much more difficult and expensive for companies to raise capital. It is in this way then that the *general level* of market yields and security prices on the Stock Exchange may be said to act as a macro-barometer

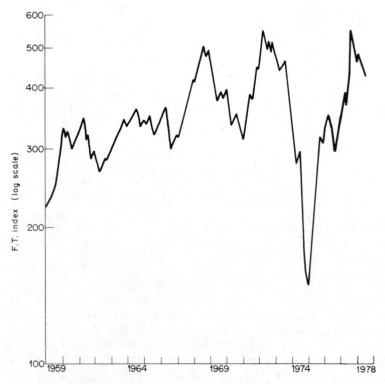

Fig. 5.2. The movement of shares: bull markets and bear markets.

for the investment prospects of the economy as a whole. It is important to note that the level of stock market prices usually anticipates or discounts expected *future* developments: it does not necessarily reflect the *current* situation – for this was very probably discounted in the level of security prices at some earlier stage.

The question may be asked, How reliable is the stock market as a macro-barometer? Clearly, if for whatever reasons it were a misleading economic indicator the implications might be serious – particularly from the point of view of government policy which would take into account the state of the stock market as one indicator, among several, of the trend of economic activity. In practice, the London stock market has had an uncanny knack of anticipating – generally about a year or so in advance – the trend of economic activity in the UK. This then raises the interesting question of whether the great share collapse of 1973–1974 was an indicator of a correspondingly severe future business recession – or merely a false alarm. At the time of writing it is still too early to give an answer. The 1973–1974 crash is examined in Chapter 7.

The Stock Exchange and company take-overs

We saw that the pricing of securities on the stock market helps to shape the uses to which new investment finance is put. In addition, what is not always appreciated is that . . . 'another important function which the stock market may reasonably be expected to perform is to ensure that the *existing* assets of firms are also most profitably utilized'[1]. What is being referred to there is company *take-overs*. By a take-over we mean a situation in which one company, by purchasing a majority of another company's shares, gains control of it. If the two firms in question combine to form a new company, we often speak of a *merger*. Formerly, it was possible for one company to take over another by purchasing its shares piece-meal on the Stock Exchange. In due course the time would come when the one company had acquired a controlling interest in the other's share capital and could then show its hand. Nowadays any company planning to take over another company, is required, under the terms of the *Take-over Code* (p. 78) to make a direct formal offer to the other company's shareholders. Generally, it will need to pitch its offer sufficiently above the current market value of the other company's

---

[1] Ajit Singh, op. cit. p. 2.

63

shares for it to be really attractive to its shareholders. If enough shareholders accept the offer – which may be in cash, or in shares – the bidding company will gain control. If not, the take-over bid lapses and the two companies go their separate ways.

There are a number of possible motives for take-overs:

(a) A company's directors may want the prestige (and salaries) which come from running a large firm.

(b) A take-over may be part of a defensive strategy, directed at securing a company's sources of supply, or markets.

(c) A take-over may be aimed at suppressing competition and establishing a monopoly situation in the market for a given good or service.

(d) What we are concerned with in our present context however is a fourth possible situation, in which a company with dynamic management wishes to take over the running of another company whose assets are, in its view, being used inefficiently and unprofitably. In these circumstances, the stock market value of the latter company's shares will tend to be rather low, which will make it additionally attractive as a cheap buy for a more efficiently run company, which should be able to use its assets better and so increase the earnings and market value of the shares.

In fact, it could be argued that take-overs provide a double discipline towards ensuring an efficient use of existing company assets. First, successful take-overs may be expected to take assets out of the hands of relatively inefficient management and place them with more competent management. Secondly the threat of a take-over may keep a management on its toes – as Dr. Johnson himself might perhaps have said, 'Depend upon it, Sir, when a man knows his company is to be bid for in a fortnight, it concentrates his mind wonderfully.'

One disagreeable feature of take-overs is that the impact of re-organizing the newly acquired company's assets often falls on people who were in no way directly responsible for its fortunes – particularly redundant employees who may be summarily sacked and find considerable difficulty in getting new employment. In the case of dismissed directors, on the other hand, the blow is likely to be cushioned by generous golden handshakes – compensation for loss of office. Even so, it is common for boards of directors to fight a take-over bid for their company very fiercely, and to seek to deter their own shareholders from accepting a rival company's offer by promising improved future earnings under their own continuing control. It is not surprising that some take-over bids have witnessed some very rough tactics, which is why the Take-over Panel was set up some years ago by the government to try to ensure better standards of behaviour.

The next question we need to ask is: Do take-overs actually achieve in practice the more efficient use of assets which might theoretically be expected? In some cases, the answer has been 'no' – the management of the controlling company, in attempting to reorganize its acquisition has bitten off more than it can chew. Thus not only may it fail to restore the fortunes of the acquired company, but managerial indigestion may also cause its own efficiency to suffer – in some respects, the background to British Leyland's difficulties in the early 1970s. Moreover, even when a take-over does appear to have improved the efficiency and profits of the acquired firm, it is hard to prove how much this is due to the impact of the new parent management, and how much to other factors, including decisions taken previously by the old management. A detailed investigation[1] carried out on take-overs which took place in Britain during the 1950s reached the following conclusions:

(a) The scale of take-overs was considerable: of the 2126 manufacturing companies (excluding steel) quoted on the Stock Exchange in 1954 more than 400 were taken over at some time in the following six years.

(b) The companies which were taken over tended to be below average in terms of size, profitability and growth. They also tended to have a higher gearing ratio (see p. 14) than other companies. However the differences in these respects between the acquired companies and the remainder were rather small, and while many unprofitable companies were not taken over, a number of very profitable companies in fact were! In statistical terms[2] most of the correlations between company size, growth, gearing and profitability were rather low.

(c) In view of (b) it was inferred that the fear of being taken over was probably not a significant stimulus to improved efficiency on

----

[1] Ajit Singh, op. cit.

[2] Readers interested in this field may care to look at B. Davies and J. Foad, *An Introduction to Statistics for Economics*, Heinemann Educational Books.

the part of slackly managed companies. (One might question whether this conclusion continued to be valid: by the late 1960s the scale of take-overs was such that the threat of being acquired was becoming an everyday fact of business life.)

(d) It was found that the companies responsible for taking over others were in general relatively large and fast-growing.

(e) There was little evidence that the profitability of companies improved after they were taken over. If anything, the controlling companies themselves tended to do rather worse than previously!

The Stock Exchange and invisible exports

Another aspect of the Stock Exchange is that the use by foreign investors of its services brings in useful invisible export receipts. Unfortunately, it is difficult to obtain really reliable estimates of such earnings. According to one estimate[1] the foreign earnings of London jobbers and brokers in 1973 were probably about £18 millions, while those from underwriting and security management were probably of a similar order. Earlier, in 1965, the London banks were earning annually about £20 millions abroad from their services, including fees for brokerage and investment advice. However it must be remembered that the entire complex of the City of London's services – the Stock Exchange, the new issue market, foreign exchange dealings, the commodity markets, insurance and so on – are interdependent, with the activities of one part of the City contributing to the earnings of the others. On this basis the London Stock Exchange plays a small but valuable part in the City's total foreign earnings, which were estimated in 1973 at £704 millions.

Oil money and the London capital market

In 1974 the London stock market found itself in a new role. At this time the United Kingdom's balance of payments on current account was in heavy deficit owing to a number of factors, including chronic domestic inflationary pressures; the continuing rise in world commodity prices; and the sharp increase in the world oil prices, which had risen from about $3 a barrel in the middle of 1973 to $10 early in 1974. The other side of the oil coin was an extraordinary rise, in the order of $60,000 millions per annum, in the oil-producing countries' earnings of foreign currency.

---

[1] *The Times*, 9 October, 1974.

Oil-producing countries such as Iran, with ambitious plans for economic development, found this oil-surplus of great benefit, since it allowed them to finance heavy imports of capital goods. For the smaller and industrially less-developed oil-producing countries however, with relatively modest import needs, these huge oil earnings presented something of a problem, since unless some positive policy were followed they would merely be transformed into sterile foreign exchange reserves. Also there was the risk that the large oil deficits of the industrial countries would provoke these individually to pursue destructive import-restricting beggar-my-neighbour policies. These in turn would damage the general prospects for international trade and hence the position of the oil-producing countries themselves. In the event, a number of oil-producing countries decided to invest some of their surplus funds in the industrial countries. They thus not only acquired useful earning assets for themselves but also at the same time helped to finance the oil deficits of the industrial oil-importing countries.

The London capital market, with its experienced and specialized institutions which are able to handle very large investment transactions, was in this respect particularly well placed. Moreover, the fall in London share prices had made a number of British companies attractive take-over prospects for foreign capital. The influx of oil money into Britain began when the Abu Dhabi Investment Board bought a £36 millions stake in the Commercial Union's head office property in London. Then, about the same time in 1974, the Kuwait Ministry of Finance and Oil made a £107 millions cash bid for the St Martins property group, which owns a number of high quality London properties such as Tintagel House, The Metropolitan Police Block and Adelaide House. The Kuwait bid was substantially more than a previous £86 millions offer, in shares, by a British company, Commercial Union.

The Kuwait bid for St Martins led for a time to a general rise in the stock market values of property companies. This in turn helped to reduce somewhat the difficulties of the financial firms and institutions – such as the fringe banks (operating often in high-risk business outside the main clearing bank system), the pension funds, the insurance companies and the investment trusts – whose finances had suffered from the collapse in property values (see Chapter 7). The inflow of oil funds also gave a certain amount of support to the pound sterling, which, for a time, strengthened on the foreign exchange market. It remained to be seen, however, how far this investment of oil funds would go, and to what extent it would provide stable long-term finance for Britain's business sector in general, as opposed to the property scene in particular. It must be stressed that the role of the London Stock Exchange in absorbing Arab oil funds was in quantitative terms at this time quite small. To what extent it would provide a substantial source of business finance for Britain was unproven.

European opportunities for the London capital market

It is not possible in a short book such as this, to make a comparative study of the capital markets of individual European countries, or examine in detail the extent to which the City of London might be able to extend its activities into them. What we shall do therefore is look at the West German capital market, which exemplifies some of the characteristic features of most of the European capital markets, and use this as a base from which to draw some conclusions about London's prospects in Europe.

Bank borrowing in West Germany

Turning first to sources of finance in West Germany, we find that retained finance, in the form of profits and accumulated appreciation funds, is a key item. However, recent years have seen a reduction in the profit margins of West German businesses due, amongst other things, to increasing wage-cost pressures and to the successive increases in the exchange rate of the German mark, which have periodically reduced (for a time) the international competitiveness of German products. Increasingly, in consequence, many German firms have been forced into greater dependence on external finance – notably bank borrowing. By 1970 for example the three biggest West German commercial banks were providing between them 28 per cent of manufacturing industry's total finance, while the savings banks were contributing a further 26 per cent, much of which was for fixed assets. The banks have thus over the years been able to acquire a very substantial amount of ownership, and even control, of private industry. An important influence in this respect has been the West German government's policy of encouraging long-term savings deposits through generous tax advantages. Another factor has been the readiness of West German banks to raise finance by issuing their own medium-term bonds to the public. West German banks also act both as issuing houses for companies raising capital on the new issue market, and as brokers and dealers on the stock exchanges.

However the increased role of bank finance in West German business has brought problems with it. One of these is that many German firms have developed a highly geared capital structure. In a period of expanding business earnings this may be acceptable but in a recession it could lead to severe financial pressures. Another difficulty is that the German banks, as major shareholders, in industry may face

> a conflict of interests between different functions carried out by a bank which makes loans and advances, holds controlling equity interests, owns a share portfolio, belongs to a new issue syndicate, manages unit trusts and also acts as private portfolio manager or adviser. . . . Nor should one forget the problems which may arise from banks simultaneously acting as stock exchange dealers and as holders of securities.[1]

The new issue market in West Germany

West German companies also raise capital by means of security issues on the open capital market. Compared with Britain (and the United States) the West German new issue market has, for several reasons, traditionally played a small part in financing German business.

(a) One factor has been the reluctance of the German public to invest in business securities – a reflection, partly, of Germany's mixed political and social fortunes in the past, including depression and hyperinflation, war and military occupation.

(b) Nor do the West German pension funds and insurance companies invest much of their funds in company securities: in the early 1960s these institutions supplied only 10 per cent of the external finance of West German firms – in Britain the corresponding figure was 40 per cent.

(c) A third factor has been the weakness of the capital market institutions in West Germany. This in turn partly reflects the unwillingness of the big financial institutions to market their holdings of company securities, and so allow a wider spread of share ownership by the general public. Consequently the German stock exchanges are

---

[1] *The Development of a European Capital Market*, E.E.C. Commission, November, 1966, p. 242 (quoted in *Lloyds Bank Review*, July 1967, p. 25).

still small and their dealings are dominated by the banks; there is also a lack of specialized issuing houses and underwriters, such as exist in London.

(d) A fourth factor has been the poor state of company accounting in West Germany as well as in continental Europe generally:

> A more liberal distribution of the equity will, in turn, require major improvements in the disclosure of corporate information in a consolidated and standardized form. This is one of the strongest recommendations of the Segré report, which also contains a valuable model of a detailed prospectus for every kind of new issue. From this there follows a requirement for more and specific legislation. The status, standards and practices of auditors and accountants will also need to be raised to inspire confidence in their independence, accuracy and judgement. All this will compel companies and their financial advisers to take a more realistic view of their financial structures and their financing needs . . .[1]

The sum effect of these four factors has been that investments in West Germany (and the continent generally) have not been subjected to the full discipline of a wide and sensitive new issue market and stock exchange dealings system.

By the 1970s however the situation in West Germany seemed to be improving: German investors were now beginning to take more interest in stock exchange dealings, due partly to the efforts of the banks to make share-buying more popular. The rapid expansion of the secondary securities market was in turn enabling companies to raise some of the finance required for heavy investment programmes. The reader may ask how it is, taking the post-war period as a whole, that West Germany has been able to achieve such remarkable economic success with indifferent financial institutions. The answer would be found outside her financial system: in efficient management, good labour relations, a tradition of excellent industrial design, and many other factors. Nevertheless it was possible, regarding the West German business and financial scene in 1973, to come to the conclusion that the tightness of the capital markets and the falling level of profits was leading to a dangerous dependence on bank finance, and indeed bank control.[2]

---

[1] *Lloyds Bank Review*, July 1967, p. 20.

[2] Frank Vogl, *German Business after the Economic Miracle*, Macmillan, 1973, p. 169.

THE SIGNIFICANCE OF THE STOCK EXCHANGE

The prospects for a European capital market

Although the capital markets of the Western European countries differ from one another in a number of respects they are – with the exception of that of the Netherlands – underdeveloped. Moreover there are, even within the European Economic Community, still government restrictions on the movement of capital between countries. Hence it is likely to be a good many years before it is possible for a unified and efficient West European capital market to emerge. If the conditions are right and that time does come the London capital market institutions – broking and jobbing firms, issuing houses, underwriters, and the specialized financial intermediaries – could have an excellent opportunity to expand their activities further into Europe:

> If an efficient European capital market is, therefore, to be successfully developed a network of transactions or connections will hardly do the trick. First, far greater emphasis than hitherto will need to be placed on developing the domestic secondary markets [that is, stock exchanges] for domestically listed securities. And, secondly, this is almost bound to lead eventually to the predominance of one centre . . . given that sterling remains strong, that centre will in the end almost certainly be the City of London . . .
>
> By the same token, it is hard to see how and where a genuine European capital market can develop if the U.K. does not join [the EEC] or how the various existing markets within the Community will turn into genuine capital markets with genuine investment institutions without the competitive pressures which the combined forces of the City would exert. It is at least arguable that London's financial institutions and markets will powerfully influence their future course, more powerfully, perhaps, than any policy recommendations, or reforms. London alone, it seems, is in a position to provide the active catalyst for developing Europe's capital market, but this is more likely to be so from within the Community than from without.[1]

This prediction was partly borne out by developments following the setting up of the European Free Trade Area, which allowed member countries access to the London capital market. The 1960s saw a number of Scandinavian municipalities raising capital funds in London. In addition several private investment projects in EFTA countries were financed by London institutions, often in non-sterling funds. Now that the UK has decided to remain in

---

[1] *Lloyds Bank Review*, July 1967, p. 28.

71

the EEC, London could be able to expand its European business substantially.

The key condition in the extract quoted above is, of course 'provided that sterling remains strong'. Unfortunately Britain's balance of payments in recent years has been anything but strong[1] and given a continuation of the ineffective government policies of much of the post-war period, the pound seems likely to continue weak. If so, the missed opportunities of the City of London will no doubt be taken up by Amsterdam,[2] Frankfurt, Paris or some other continental centre.

[1] See Brinley Davies, *The UK and the World Monetary System*, Heinemann Educational Books, 1975.

[2] A pioneer in 'traded options' (see p. 56).

6
SOME CRITICISMS OF THE LONDON STOCK MARKET

Inadequate information

In Chapters 4 and 5 we were looking at the workings and significance of the Stock Exchange. In this chapter we shall be asking how effectively it performs its role. We shall begin by considering the assertion that the London stock market approximates to a perfect market for securities. One key condition for such a market is that all the buyers and sellers on the market should have a similar and sufficient amount of information. In the case of the stock market, however, there are two important areas where the information available to the investor falls short of this.[1] The first area is that of company accounts where there are major information defects:

(a) The amount of information contained in company accounts is, in spite of the increased disclosure requirements of the 1967 Companies Acts, inadequate from an investment analysis viewpoint and falls far short of what is available for example in the United States.

(b) Consequently there is also considerable scope for unscrupulous companies to use their accounts so as to conceal the fundamental facts about their financial position.

(c) Company accounts are invariably out of date, in the sense that they are presented some months after the period which they cover.

(d) The practice of each company having its own individual accounting year makes it difficult to compare the performance and prospects of different companies.

It has therefore been suggested that company accounts in this country should by law be improved as follows:[2]

1. The profit and loss statement should include the actual cost of goods sold, including fixed costs such as rent. It should also give a cumulative record of accrued liabilities and prepayments, and a record of bad debts incurred.

---

[1] R. J. Briston, op. cit., chapter 9.

[2] R. J. Briston, op. cit., p. 328.

2. The balance sheet should include full details concerning sales of fixed assets, including their book values and the actual proceeds.

3. The presentation and timing of company accounts should be fully standardized so as to make possible valid comparisons between the records of different companies.

The other main area of poor information concerns the Stock Exchange itself, which has been criticized for providing the investing public with far too little information about dealings. The Stock Exchange *Daily Official List* was intended to give a record of daily business in each share. In fact, the marketing of bargains by jobbers was voluntary; the prices quoted were not separated into those for purchases and for sales; the actual quantities bought and sold were not recorded – merely the number of deals; and the information only covered deals made up to 2.15 p.m.! It was not until 1974 that reliable daily figures on dealings were at last made available to the investing public.

The less information there is available to investors, both with regard to company accounts and to stock market dealings, the easier it is for individuals who do have access to key information, to undertake successful dealings at the expense of the general investor. For example, individual members of jobbing and broking firms, knowing the immediate movement of price changes and dealing in a particular security, may be able to move in and out of the market and make quick speculative gains before the general investing public has had time to react at all. Similarly a company employee having access to confidential accounts may (illegally) exploit this information by making stock market deals at the expense of other investors.

The decline in stock market competition

A second major criticism of the London Stock market is that its effectiveness has suffered due to the considerable decline in competition on it. As a result, it is now far from justifying the former claim of being a perfect market in which the activities of a large number of competing buyers and sellers result in an equilibrium price which none of them individually is able to influence. Turning first to the investment side we find that, while there are certainly large numbers of small investors involved, a high proportion of dealings volume is nowadays accounted for by a relatively few institutional investors (see p. 45). It would in this context therefore be more accurate to describe the investment side of the stock market as oligopolistic, rather than purely competitive.

Secondly, dealings have been falling into the hands of fewer and fewer jobbers. It is therefore no longer always true that a broker dealing in a particular security on behalf of a client is in a position to do business with a number of competing jobbers. While there were, for example, over 300 jobbing firms in 1930, by 1971 the number of jobbing firms was down to only 36. In the dark days of 1974 bankruptcy and mergers reduced the total still further, and by the end of the year there were only six *major* jobbing firms remaining. In 1978 90 per cent of the jobbing business was performed by the biggest four firms. Since each jobber specializes in a particular range of securities, the number dealing in any particular security is nowadays commonly as little as two or three – and may even be only one. Moreover, some jobbers share business through what is known as joint books, which further reduces competition.

As a result partly of declining competition, jobbers turns' have tended to widen, and dealing costs increase. Would the adoption on the London Stock Exchange of the New York dealing system increase jobbing competition and reduce dealing costs? This question is examined next.

The New York dealing system
The London Stock Exchange is the only major stock market which operates on the basis of a jobbing/broking system. On the New York exchange, which is the busiest stock market in the world, dealings take place through brokers and *specialists*. The specialists resemble (in some respects only) the London jobbers and are organized into firms of up to nine members, each firm being given, by the Exchange's Board of Governors, responsibility for a range of up to a dozen or so securities. When a New York broker gets an order from a client – for example to purchase a share – he goes to the post where the share is traded. If his order is for the best ruling market price, an auction takes place between other dealers who are also at the same post. Some of these will be brokers; others may be specialists seeking to unload shares which they have been holding on their books. The broker in question will then give his client's order to the dealer offering the lowest price.

If, however, his client's order is for a specific price the broker will place it directly with a specialist. If the specialist already has

75

the share on his books he will be in a position to execute the order forthwith. If this is not possible he will enter it in his book and, like a London jobber, carry out the order in due course.

The New York specialist thus wears a number of hats. First (like a London jobber) he acts as a principal by using his capital to buy, hold or sell, at a profit, securities on his own account. Secondly (and unlike a London jobber) he sometimes acts as an agent for another broker – he is a kind of broker's broker. Thirdly, a New York specialist is allowed to undertake direct broker dealings with the investing public. On the two broker functions he receives the appropriate brokerage commission.

An assessment of the New York system

The chief danger of the New York system is that the specialist may face a conflict of interest between his duty as an agent to buy and sell on the best terms for his client, and his motivation as a principal to deal in securities at a profit on his own behalf. No matter how effective the overseeing powers of the stock exchange authorities may be, it is difficult to see how the investor can avoid being subject to some risk in this respect.

As regards cost-effectiveness there is probably little difference between the London and New York systems in regard to inactive securities (those which are infrequently dealt in). In either case the jobber or specialist in question will need to adopt an appropriate dealing margin to cover his costs. However in the case of those securities which are actively dealt in, margins tend to be wider in the London system, on account of the decline in jobbing competition there. On the New York stock market, on the other hand, the auctioning procedure ensures that the specialists face keen competition from the brokers, and this helps to keep dealing margins at a minimum. (It is worth noting in this respect that on most of the provincial stock exchanges in Britain, brokers are in fact allowed to perform the functions of jobbers).

Although there are at· present no plans to adopt a New York two-tier system for the London Stock Exchange, other methods of making dealings more efficient are being tried or considered. One was the introduction by the outside institutions early in 1974, of the Ariel broker-to-broker computer system. This was estimated in 1974 to be doing business at an annual rate of over £100 millions, and to have taken away about one per cent of the jobbers' total share business, and two per cent of their very profitable institutional business. Secondly outside firms – such as acceptance houses – have been allowed to take up to a 10 per cent financial stake in jobbing firms, the idea being to increase the amount of capital available for jobbers so that they can deal in a wider range of securities. Another proposal which has been under consideration is to allow jobbers and brokers to pool their financial resources by merging into dual capacity firms, whilst continuing to keep their dealing functions quite separate. Moreover bankruptcies around 1974 eliminated a number of the presumably less efficient stock exchange firms, whilst mergers between those remaining were aimed at financial economies and improved efficiency.

Dishonest stock market practices

It has sometimes been possible for Stock Exchange dealers, by applying a concerted selling or buying pressure on a share to push its market price to an artificially low or high level. Provided the market is willing to support the new price, they would then be able to make a large profit by reversing their earlier dealings. For example, in 1964 a number of members were suspended by the Stock Exchange Council in connection with dealings in the shares of the firm of H. W. Philips, the price of which rose over a period of 18 months from less than 20 pence to over £1.50. Whether suspension is always a sufficient deterrent – or punishment – has been questioned.[1] Moreover, even when a member is suspended the jobbing or broking firm in question may be able to go on operating, even be indirectly controlled, by a suspended member.[2] Only in extreme circumstances has a Stock Exchange firm itself been suspended.

It can also happen that a high-level employee having confidential access to a company's accounts undertakes privileged insider dealings on the Stock Exchange. Knowing, for example, that the company's forthcoming accounts were to show an unexpected loss and that the company's share price would almost certainly fall as a result, he would be able to undertake a virtually fool-proof bear operation in the share in question. Conversely, advance knowledge of a very favourable company report would be an ideal position from which to undertake a bull operation in anticipation of a sharp

[1] R. J. Briston, op. cit., p. 119.
[2] R. J. Briston, op. cit., p. 120.

rise in the market price of the share in question. Some of the worst incidents in recent years have involved take-over bids in which company promoters have exploited their positions to undertake highly profitable share dealings at the expense of the other investors concerned. One which aroused much disquiet was that of a city financier who was accused in 1973 by the Department of Trade and Industry of grave mismanagement in connection with inter-company share dealings. This case concerned shares reportedly bought at 62 pence each and subsequently sold for personal and family gain at £8.67 each, to the detriment of company shareholders concerned.[1]

The City's Take-over Panel

It was to deal with mounting criticism after a number of suspected cases of this type, that the leading London institutions decided to publish, in 1968, a *City Code on Take-overs and Mergers*. The Code lays down voluntary rules governing take-over tactics and a Take-over Panel was set up to implement them. The main features of the Code are these:

(a) A company's directors who have decided to make a bid for another company may not buy its shares in the hope of selling them at a higher price after the take-over bid has been formally announced.

(b) Directors making a bid for another company may not make privileged and generous offers to a few of its largest shareholders only, as a short-cut method of obtaining a controlling interest.

(c) The directors of a company which is being bid for (the *offeree* company) may not attempt to frustrate a take-over merely because their own personal interests might suffer. They should not, for example, make rashly optimistic profit forecasts, in the hope of persuading their shareholders to reject a bid. Any further information which offeree directors may give about their company to their shareholders should be reliable so that they can reach an informed judgement on the proposed take-over.

(d) A company's directors may not go through the motions of announcing (and then withdrawing) a take-over bid in order to undertake speculative dealings in the shares of the offeree company. Once a company has announced a bid it is obliged to proceed with it, and it must remain open for 21 days.

[1] *The Times*, 24 July, 1974.

(e) Full details of all share dealings by the parties to the proposed take-over must be notified to the Panel.

It should be noted that the Panel does not have any legal powers to enforce the Code; it relies on voluntary self-discipline on the part of the firms concerned. It can however punish offenders in three ways. First, it can issue a public reprimand, which would involve the offenders in unfavourable publicity. Secondly, it can ask the Stock Exchange to suspend quotations of the shares of the companies in question during the period of the take-over. Thirdly, it can refer cases of possible fraud to the Board of Trade for legal action. Even so, many observers consider that the City Code – in spite of the fact that it has been several times revised to remove possible loop-holes and ambiguities – is still not effective enough. A number of recent cases have involved back-outs, where a company which has announced an offer breaks the Code by abandoning the offer. During the period of rapidly falling share prices in 1973 and 1974, a number of companies found that what at one time had seemed good take-over prospects were a little later suddenly looking very unattractive. One example of this was the St Martins decision in 1973 to increase its property assets by buying, at £4 a share, 34 per cent of the equity in the firm of Hay's Wharf. Under the terms of the Code St Martins was obliged to make a take-over bid, at the offer price of £4, for the rest of the Hay's Wharf equity. At this point, due partly to the effects of the December 1973 mini Budget, property values started to fall sharply, and the St Martins shareholders decided to vote against the increase in capital now needed to finance the bid for Hay's Wharf. The bid therefore collapsed and St Martins found itself in violation of the Take-over Code. One result of the infringement of the Code was a very unsettled market for the shares of the two companies. The Take-over Panel, when it later announced the results of its investigation, criticized the chairman of St Martins not only for being half-hearted in pursuing the take-over, but also for being 'less than candid' in his discussions with the Panel; he subsequently resigned from the St Martins board. In addition St Martins itself was deprived by the Panel of any voting power on the 34 per cent share holding which it had acquired in Hay's Wharf.

As a result of this and similar cases the effectiveness of the City's self-discipline approach on take-overs became increasingly questioned. One step advocated was the setting up of an outside regulatory body, with powers like those of the United States *Securities and*

Exchange Commission. This is an arm of the United States government which was set up to regulate security dealings on the United States stock exchanges, following the widespread dishonest practices which came to light during the 1929 Wall Street crash. The Securities and Exchange Commission's powers include the following:

(a) Any proposed new issues of securities must be registered with the Commission at least 20 days before the offer, so that it can make a searching investigation (much stricter than those applied in Britain) into the standing of the company.

(b) The Commission maintains a constant watch over stock market prices and may investigate movements indicating dishonest dealings, which can include false markets arising out of take-over situations. All quoted companies (except for the very smallest) have to report regularly to the Commission on their financial situation and on any related security dealings.

(c) Dealers who are found to have acted dishonestly can be suspended or expelled from the stock exchange or prosecuted at law for damages.

(d) *Investment advice* firms with more than 15 clients have to register with the Commission. In Britain investment counselling is still a free-range activity.

(e) The United States President may, on the advice of the Commission, close any stock exchange in the United States for a period of up to 90 days, pending an investigation by the Commission of irregular dealings.

The powers of the Commission are thus on paper very impressive; its surveyance would seem to be more penetrating than that of the Stock Exchange Council and the Take-over Panel, and its disciplinary powers tougher. In practice, though, it has not been able to prevent a number of financial scandals in the United States in recent years both in regard to take-over situations and dishonest practices generally. The effect has therefore been to strengthen the alternative view that a flexible, and informal, London-type approach may be a more effective method of checking malpractices – particularly in a community as compact and localized, and sensitive to its reputation, as the City is. In July 1974 a City Capital Markets Committee was set up under the auspices of the Bank of England to investigate this matter. It recommended in its report of December that year, a continuation of the City's self-regulation policy. The report reminded readers that investors on the London capital market are effectively protected in a number of ways: the level of company disclosure required by the Stock Exchange is higher than statutory requirements; there are Stock Exchange rules against dishonest trading; the Stock Exchange compensation fund protects investors against default by brokers; and the Take-over Panel protects the interest of shareholders in take-over situations. The Committee did however recommend that insider dealing be made a criminal defence, and subject to the normal legal processes. The chairman of the committee concluded that there was no case at all for slavish imitation of systems imported from elsewhere.[1]

The Labour Government's 1974 Green Paper on Company Law reform proposed that a Companies Commission should be set up. Although it would lack the political and parliamentary contacts which the United States Security and Exchange Commission has, its brief would be a very wide one: to control company affairs so as to protect not only the interests of shareholders, but also of employees and the community at large. It would embrace, in addition to the capital markets, the areas of banking, insurance, hire purchase and house finance.

The Office of Fair Trading and the London Stock Exchange

The question of reform of the London stock exchange came to a head in 1977 when the Office of Fair Trading placed the whole of the Stock Exchange's rules on the register of the Restrictive Practices Court. The practices likely to be examined included the following:

1. *Fixed commissions by brokers.* Minimum charges on the purchase and sale of securities are fixed by the Stock Exchange Council after consultation with investors. Brokerage charges increased substantially in London in the 1970s in contrast to the United States where minimum charges had been abolished. There, commissions on mainline tradings fell, though small investors continued to pay higher rates. The danger of competitive commissions is that they may push brokers out of business and increase the oligopoly element in the market.

2. *The ban on jobbers acting as brokers and vice versa.* We examined earlier the difficulties faced by London jobbing firms in the 1970s

---

[1] *The Times,* 18 December, 1974

81

and the decline in competition in the jobbing market. Whether the adoption of the American dual-capacity system (see p. 75) would provide a more effective market was a question likely to be explored when the London stock exchange found itself before the Restrictive Practices Court.

3. *Restrictions on broker-to-broker 'put-through' deals and the ban on deals made outside the Stock Exchange without the Council's permission.* The defence of these practices would be that specialized dealing leads to improved efficiency. Yet there is no doubt that many brokers dislike having to offer 'put-through' deals to jobbers. Equally London jobbers can suffer from not being allowed to deal directly with investment clients; a factor which lost the jobbing firm of Smith Brothers a big overseas deal in 1977. Significantly, in the United States at this time the Securities and Exchange Commission was preparing the groundwork of an integrated stock market system which would be based on new data-processing and communications methods and the probable sanctioning of 'off-beat' dealings external to the stock exchange floors.[1] The matching of buying and selling deals would then often be carried out on an office-to-office basis, rather than by floor brokers ankle deep in paper.

Whether the London exchange is ready for reform on the American scale is doubtful. But some kind of change must come. The findings of the Office of Fair Trading will be awaited with great interest.

The stock market as an investment allocator – does it really work?
We saw on p. 60 that the stock market might be expected to act as an allocator of investment resources: the market yield of a company's security tending to reflect investing opinion as to its future prospects and hence determining the cost to it of raising capital on the new issue market. This assertion is however subject to a number of assumptions:

(a) The first assumption (see p. 53) is that the effect of speculation is to stabilize the market price of shares on the stock market. If this is not so, and the operations of speculation in any given period distort the stock market, the prices and yields of company securities will be a false guide to their earnings prospects, and companies will find themselves raising capital at the wrong price.

(b) It is assumed that the stock market is always able to quote a

---

[1] *The Economist*, 25 April, 1978.

price for any company security – that there are not occasions when, due to market uncertainty and low earnings, jobbers are unwilling to commit themselves to a price. However, during the 1974 share crash there were many reports of company securities being virtually unsaleable: although jobbers often claimed that this merely reflected reluctance on the part of the investors to accept realistically low prices – particularly in the case of company debentures where, even at the best of times, marketability is often extremely thin.

(c) It is assumed *that it is possible in practice to forecast with reasonable reliability the likely future earnings of any given company*. A number of economists doubt whether this assumption is justified. They argue that the interaction of economic and other factors which affect company costs, turnover and profits are so complex, and include so many fortuitous events, that the future earnings of any company are essentially indeterminate. For example a statistical study published in 1962 by I. M. D. Little[1] aimed to show that the growth of profits per share of different companies is largely random, and that a firm's future profits cannot be successfully predicted on the basis of its past profits. On this view, investors who base their decisions on the interpretation of company accounts may believe that they are investing in firms with high-profit prospects – but in practice they are no more likely to pick a winning share than the old lady who selects her investments with a pin. It would in any case be unrealistic to expect analysts to forecast the future profits of a company, when the directors themselves are often unable to predict them with any substantial degree of accuracy.[2]

If, therefore, there is really little to choose between good and bad companies, the claim that the stock market, in conjunction with the new issue market, helps to channel investment resources into their most efficient uses, must be abandoned. To understand this point more fully let us take a case of a company which is considered by investors to have a high earnings growth potential, so that the market yield on its shares is, say, 2 per cent, thus enabling it to raise fresh equity capital very cheaply. If, in the outcome, the firm's profits and dividends do not live up to expectations the market yield on its shares will rise very considerably. Clearly, then, it did not 'deserve'

---

[1] I. M. D. Little: 'Higgledy-piggledy growth', from the *Bulletin of the Oxford Institute of Statistics*, 24 November, 1962.

[2] R. J. Briston, op. cit., p. 399.

to be able to raise share capital at around 2 per cent, but should really have paid much more. According to Little, (and others), this type of situation is in fact common: the price which companies pay for external capital often bears little relation to the efficiency with which they are likely to use it.

This view has however been questioned on two grounds. First, the interpretation of data by statistical techniques is itself inexact and investigations like the one above have themselves been criticized (by other statisticians) as misleading and unreliable! Secondly, the conclusions above simply conflict with common sense and experience – namely, that some companies are well-managed and do operate profitably by reacting efficiently to changing circumstances and opportunities (such as Tesco in the 1960s), while others (such as British Leyland in the 1970s) are dogged by difficulties which their management seems unable to solve, with the result that their performance and profitability persistently decline.

Retained earnings and the role of the capital market

In recent years, retained profits plus depreciation funds, together with bank credit, have accounted for far and away the main part of British companies' capital funds (table 6.1). Consequently, it is argued, the role of the London capital market has now become negligible.

Table 6.1   Domestic sources of capital funds of industrial and commercial companies in the UK, 1969, 1973 and 1977

		£ million	
	1969	*1973*	*1977*
Undistributed income	3,251	6,633	11,362
Capital transfers:			
Investment grants	556	227	33
Other	42	146	282
Bank borrowing	664	4,505	3,085
Other loans and mortgages	211	893	162
Capital issues by quoted companies:			
Ordinary shares	177	98	723
Debentures and preference	335	51	−84
Total	5,236	12,553	15,563

Source: *Financial Statistics* HMSO, 1978.

Actually, table 6.1 exaggerates the role of new issues, since it includes capital issues designed merely to finance take-over bids. It is probable that net capital issues have amounted to no more than about 10 per cent of total business finance since 1970 and probably as little as one per cent in 1973 and 1974. The factors making for heavy company indebtedness to banks in recent years are many and complex, and are examined in the next chapter. On the question of retained finance, one reason why many companies avoid where possible using the new issue market is that they are able (when their earnings permit) to plough back profits into investment with relatively little scrutiny on the part of shareholders. Capital issues on the other hand are subject to much more stringent scrutiny. Secondly, expanding earnings per share via re-investment of profits is considered to be to the benefit of many shareholders, compared with dividend distributions. The reason for this is that investors pay capital gains tax when they dispose of shares at an increased market price, compared with the much higher income tax rates many of them would have to pay on dividends. Thirdly, companies often apparently regard retained profits as free finance, whereas issues of securities, on which interest or dividends must be paid, are seen as dear finance.[1] This is a false notion, since it leaves out of account the opportunity cost of reinvested earnings: that is, the rate of return which the company might have received on its own funds if it had invested them externally – for example, in government bonds. Nevertheless, at least until the financial crisis of 1973–1974 set in, retained earnings continued to be the dominant source of finance for most companies.

Since, then, so many companies depend heavily on bank borrowing and retained finance, it is inferred that they are largely immune to the discipline of the capital market barometer, with respect to their financial requirements, apart from exceptional instances where very large amounts of capital are needed. However, it may be argued that measuring the relative *quantities* of finance which companies obtain from different sources, misses the main point about the value of the open capital market, which is the *quality* of the finance which it makes available. For if there were no capital market, firms might be starved of long-term investment finance at crucial periods of their development. In addition, finance obtained through share-issues on the capital market has a very important advantage, compared with

[1] R. J. Briston, op. cit., p. 130.

other forms of finance. This is that during a period of low profits, or losses, a company may waive the dividends and so reduce the total claims on its financial resources. Provided therefore that the capital market recovers from its low ebb of 1974, it would be wrong to understate its contribution to business finance. In the event the later 1970s were to witness useful recovery in equity issues (see p. 109).

7
THE LONDON STOCK MARKET IN THE 1970s

Background to the crash of 1973–4

During 1971 and the first part of 1972 the prices of most shares quoted on the London Stock Exchange rose substantially and in May 1972 the *Financial Times* ordinary share index of thirty leading shares (1935 base = 100) reached an all-time high of 543.6. This share boom reflected optimism on the part of investors about the prospects for a continued expansion of the economy (and company profits), now that the Conservative government had shown itself committed, under the Chancellorship of Anthony Barber, to a dash for growth via monetary and fiscal expansion. In the latter part of 1972, however, there were indications that the economic boom might be slowing down, or even coming to an end. A domestic danger signal was the appearance of labour shortages and increasing inflation. An external signal was the widening current account deficit on the balance of payments, associated with a weakening of sterling. Investors now began to feel that direct pressures on profits might soon come into play – particularly rising unit costs for wages and dearer imported materials. It was also feared that the government might have to impose restraints on profits and dividends as part of any prices and incomes policy for inflation.

These doubts about the future economic climate turned out to be

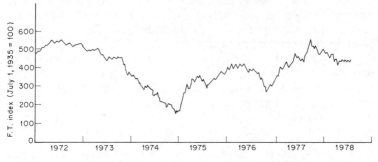

Fig. 7.1. Share prices since the late 1960s.

justified, for although in 1973 many companies continued to record good profits (on paper at least – p. 92) by 1974 a considerable decline in profits was taking place. During these two years there took place an unprecedented collapse in share prices and by early January 1975 the *Financial Times* ordinary share index had fallen to 146. This was the lowest share level for twenty years, and, allowing for the rise in prices in the post-war period, probably the lowest in real terms since the *Financial Times* share index began in 1935.

Effects of the stock market crash of 1973–4
The stock market crash had a number of adverse effects:

(a) The fall in share prices and, to a lesser extent, debenture prices, was associated with a very large rise in market yields. By August 1974 the yield on Unilever ordinary shares was 5·7 per cent, while on I.C.I. shares it was 8·4 per cent and on British Leyland shares 23·7 per cent! The average market share yield was now 11 per cent, compared with 5 per cent and $6\frac{1}{2}$ per cent respectively in the last two bear markets of 1970 and 1966. Similarly the average price-earnings ratio of quoted shares in August 1974 was less than five, compared with 12 in the 1966 bear market. As the share collapse continued, so market yields of company securities continued to rise, and their price-earnings ratios fell. The effect of this situation was to make it very expensive for companies to raise new capital on the open market. In fact, in the first three months of 1974 only one new public issue took place and even that was undersubscribed! And when Commercial Union made a rights offer of shares late in 1974 it had to offer a prospective yield of 17 per cent to float the issue. Taking 1974 as a whole, the contribution of new security issues to business finance was probably less than one per cent. Many companies were therefore forced into an undue, and expensive, dependence upon short- and medium-term bank credit.
(b) The collapse in security prices accentuated the general mood of pessimism about the state of the economy and hence the disinclination of companies to invest – though in the outcome most companies' investment plans[1] held up surprisingly well during 1974.
(c) The reduced value of company securities held as assets by banks,

---

[1] For a general analysis of the determinants of investment see J. R. Davies and S. Hughes, *Investment in the British Economy*, Heinemann Educational Books, 1976.

insurance companies and other financial institutions led in due course to constant and unsettling rumours of impending bankruptcies among them. Eventually, rumour became fact, for a number of 'fringe' banks and insurance companies were forced into liquidation during 1974. This increased the danger that depositors and other creditors might panic and withdraw funds from the banks and institutions and so trigger off a general financial crash. Moreover the greatly reduced value of equities and debentures deposited by many smaller firms as collateral for bank loans, was undermining their ability to secure further loan finance. A case in point was that of Burmah Oil, which on account of the fall in its asset portfolio, was forced late in 1974 to sell off its North Sea oil investments.

(d) It is estimated[1] that two-thirds of households in Britain save directly or indirectly in the form of share holdings. Many ordinary families who had invested, however modestly, in shares or in unit- and investment-trusts, found by the end of 1974 that – assuming they wished to sell – a large part of their savings had been wiped out. At the peak of share prices in 1972 the total market value of all shares was £66,000 millions; in December 1974 it was only £16,000 millions. Also the retirement prospects of people depending on pension funds were threatened by the continuing inflation which at the end of 1974 was approaching an annual rate of 20 per cent, and by the poor outlook for share earnings (so much so, that the British Railways Pension Fund was reported to be investing in Old Masters paintings as well as shares!)

The decline in company profitability in the 1970s

The background to the stock market crash of 1973 and 1974 lay in the fact that the profitability of British business was falling – and seemed likely, in the view of many investors, to go on falling further. Hence the apparently well-established case for investing in company shares as a long-term hedge against inflation – that is, an inflation-proof form of saving – was becoming increasingly doubtful. A good example of the loss of faith in shares was the action of the various investment trusts belonging to the Slater Walker financial group which in 1974 began systematically to sell company securities and invest in liquid assets, such as local authority yearling bonds and bank deposits; and in gold shares and gold coins (Krugerrands). (There

---

[1] *Sunday Telegraph*, 15 December 1974.

may have been a tactical element here, with a re-purchase of shares not being ruled out if, in due course, market prices started to improve).

Basically there were two elements in the falling profit situation. The first of these was a declining long-term trend in business profits which had been taking place since the 1960s. The second consisted of a number of special factors making for falling profits and a tight company liquidity situation in the particular circumstances of 1973 and 1974. Let us begin by examining the long-term trend in profits. Figure 7.2 shows three measures of the profitability of industrial and commercial companies. Although rates of return are subject to appreciable cyclical fluctuation, the rates of return calculated by valuing assets at current replacement cost (see p. 92) show a steady declining trend in the 1960s and 1970s.

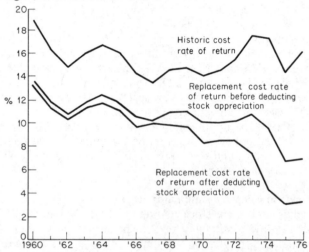

Fig. 7.2. Company profitability since the 1960's.
Source: *Bank of England Quarterly Bulletin*, Dec. 1974.

(Interestingly, there is also evidence of a decline in business profitability in a number of other advanced industrial countries.)

Specific factors affecting the trend of profits

(a) *Rising wage costs*
It is not possible in a short book such as this to explore in detail the complex factors which shaped the general movement of the

90

British economy, including the level of business profits, in the 1960s and 1970s. However, a number of factors can be briefly mentioned, the first of these being the effects of *wage-cost inflation*. Most students of economics are aware that – unlike the proverbial leopard – inflation in recent years does seem to have changed its spots. Up to the late 1960s inflation in Britain, and in many other countries, was generally taken to be mainly the result of an excessive growth of aggregate demand pulling up the general level of prices of goods and services. Claims for increased wages and salaries were then interpreted as being a response (under conditions, often, of extreme full employment) by worker-groups attempting to defend the real purchasing power of their wages. In terms of this explanation there was no reason necessarily to expect inflation to put any general pressure on the profits of companies. In fact, if incomes from employment were slow to react to rising prices, the effect of inflation would, other things being equal, be to increase the general level of companies' profits (though there would, of course, still be individual cases of unsuccessful companies experiencing falling profits).

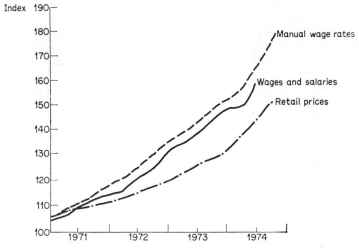

Fig. 7.3. Wages and prices in the early 1970s (1970 = 100).
Source: *Economic Trends*, HMSO, 1974.

In recent years, however, Britain, and many other countries, seem to have experienced a new source of rising prices, namely rising

91

wage-costs initiated by aggressive wage bargaining, even in periods when unemployment has been relatively high (such as 1971 in Britain), and worker militancy might have been expected to weaken. One effect of the new situation has been that companies' wage-costs per unit of output have tended to be pushed up at a faster rate than companies themselves have been able, in a competitive environment, to raise their prices.

That is why, on this view of inflation, there has been a falling trend of profits in recent years, and the prospect of a continuing decline. The effect of falling profits is not only that there is an increasing lack of internal finance; there is also a reduced incentive for investors to take new security issues by companies. As a result many firms are being pushed into an increasing reliance on bank finance and on official or semi-official bodies such as Finance for Industry (p. 105) and the proposed National Enterprise Board (p. 129).

(b) *The taxation of profits and inflation accounting*

The rapid inflation of recent years, taken in conjunction with traditional accounting techniques, has led to many companies facing considerable tax difficulties. For traditional accounting methods are based on the assumption that the value of money is constant: all pounds in a company's balance sheets and income statements are assumed to be equal, regardless of the particular year to which they relate. When prices change rapidly, traditional accounts are therefore blind to the fact that a pound spent by a company in 1975 is not the same as a pound that was spent (or earned) in 1965. One case in point is the tax treatment of depreciation. As a company's fixed assets wear out, it is allowed under the tax laws to accumulate funds free of tax to replace these assets, on the assumption that the new assets will cost no more than the old assets did. However, in a period of rapid inflation a machine bought ten years ago for £8,000 might now cost, say, £20,000 to replace. Hence the company in question will need to find, over and above its £8,000 depreciation allowance, a further £12,000 out of its (taxed) profits to finance the replacement of the machine.

Another case in point concerns companies' current assets in the form of stocks. In a period of rising prices, the present money value of a company's stock may be £2 million compared with an original purchase cost of say £1½ million. The company in question will then be taxed as having made a profit of £½ million even though in real terms the value of its current assets has probably remained much the same.

This problem is further affected by the particular accounting conventions governing the measurement of a company's stock operations. The basic difficulty is that of identifying the turn-over in a number of identical items of stock – for example bales of wood pulp purchased at different times and at different prices. It is assumed by British accountants and tax authorities that when an item is taken out of stock it is the one in stock which was first bought. In a period of rising prices this *first in, first out* (FIFO) method means that the item used is assumed to be one which cost least and which therefore shows most profit. There are a number of countries, including the United States, where a different convention, the *last in, first out* (LIFO) method is used, in which the item used is assumed to be the latest to enter stock. The effect at a time of rising prices is here to reduce the amount of stock profit. It has been calculated that the adoption of a LIFO method of stock valuation could have saved British companies in 1974 about £1,000 millions of tax in total.

The 1974 November budget did give some *ad hoc* tax relief in this respect (p. 100) and pointed clearly towards the adoption of some form of inflation accounting for stock operations in the near future.

Ideally a new accounting system would need to reflect the economist's view that the concept of profit should take account of the cost of maintaining the earning power of a business – including the cost of more expensive stocks in a time of rising prices. It should, however, be noted that the value of many companies' stocks in recent years has, on account of much higher primary product prices, risen even faster than prices in general. So even on full inflation-accounting basis most would have continued to pay some tax on stock appreciation. Secondly, inflation, by expanding the money value of stocks, increases the amount of working capital required to finance stocks, and thereby adds to the financial pressures on companies.

Taking into account, then, both the factors we have now examined (fixed-asset depreciation and stock appreciation) it can be seen that the effect of rapid inflation combined with traditional accounting has been to exaggerate very greatly the profits which many companies in Britain have appeared – on paper – to be making,

93

and hence the amounts of corporation tax which they have been required to pay.

A further dangerous side-effect of the situation has been that some companies may have been misled by large paper profits into over-estimating their financial resources and so distributing more to their shareholders, or paying more to their employees, than they could really afford.

Moreover, the degree of distortion resulting from traditional accounting at a time of rapid inflation varies from company to company. For example, although around 1974 many manufacturing companies found that their true profits were badly overstated, the profits of many property companies were actually *understated*. This was because these companies held little or no stocks; owned fixed assets, in the form of buildings which – until recently – had been appreciating, and, being highly geared, they found that the real interest burden on their past borrowing was constantly being reduced by the effects of inflation.

It was calculated that the use in 1974 of inflation accounting on average would have halved the reported earnings of the major electrical companies.[1] Other sectors which would have been significantly helped in this way were oil companies, the motor industry, the engineering companies, shipping and tobacco companies. Proper inflation accounting would conversely probably have doubled the reported earnings of the major property companies and increased by 20 per cent the reported earnings of breweries and entertainment companies.

Table 7.1 Approximate percentage change in the 1974 earnings of selected companies using inflation accounting.

	%
MEPC[2]	+160
Trust Houses Forte	+60
Bass Charrington	+19
Marks & Spencers	+10
Tesco	−5
Courtaulds	−45
British Leyland	−100
International Computers	−300

[1] *Sunday Telegraph*, 19 May, 1974.

[2] Formerly Metropolitan Estate and Property Corporation.

94

On account of these anomalies, it was becoming very difficult in the early 1970s to make reliable comparisons of the performance and prospects of different companies and sectors in the economy, and the role of the London capital markets was thus further weakened.

Back in the 1950s the Dutch electrical firm of Philips introduced its own system of inflation accounting, in which all its financial accounts are converted into money units of current purchasing power in the form of present-day prices. This helps the management of Philips to assess clearly its business operations (though Philips continues, of course, to pay company tax on the same basis as other companies operating in Britain and using traditional accounting). An important first step was taken in 1974 towards a possible general introduction of inflation accounting in Britain, when the government-appointed Sandilands committee published a set of provisional inflation accounting rules for the guidance of firms.

The essence of inflation accounting is to replace historical cost with some notion of present cost. In the *current purchasing power* method (CCP), assets and liabilities in company accounts are revalued with reference to a general index of inflation such as, in the UK, the General Index of Retail Prices. Originally the accounting profession, through its own committee, recommended a CCP method. The snag with CCP is that the current value of any particular asset may prove to have moved quite out of line with prices in general. The Sandilands committee (which, incidentally, contained a number of non-accountants) opted for a system of current cost accounting (CCA). This method calls for assets to be recorded at their 'value to the business' on the basis either of a specific inflation index for each industry or an individual assessment of each asset in the company account.

In 1977 the Morpeth committee, representing the main accounting organs in Britain, also opted for a CCA approach to inflation accounting similar to that proposed by Sandilands. Unlike Sandilands, Morpeth recommended that an allowance should be made for inflation effects on monetary items in the accounts such as cash and borrowing – an important consideration in the case of banks and financial institutions. The guidelines offered on this by Morpeth were however vague and subjective. Moreover the Morpeth instructions for valuing plant and machinery in the balance sheet were widely felt to be unnecessarily complicated. It came as no surprise when, in 1977, a postal vote among accountants rejected the Morpeth proposals. In response, an official accounting committee conceded that there would

95

now be no introduction of inflation accounting unless it was generally acceptable to the accountancy profession. We can perhaps leave a final comment on the 1977 position to *The Economist*:[1]

> This could well ensure that Britain sees no system of inflation accounting for years ahead. Company managers have a fair idea of the impact of inflation on the businesses they run, but do not have to share this fascinating information with shareholders, creditors and employees. Why should they make their lives more difficult by helping people monitor their performance? The backwoodsmen of the profession will always argue for an easy life. And the academics will argue for ever.
>
> Unless the accountancy profession shows itself willing to justify the privileges it enjoys by exhibiting high professional standards, its days in the private sector are numbered. High professional standards, in this instance, imply the best possible inflation accounting system as soon as possible, as opposed to the one dictated by the profession's least able members, and its paymasters in industry.

It has not been possible within the limits of this book to discuss all the implications of inflation accounting. What is important for our present purpose is to understand how traditional accounting and tax assessment, combined with rapid inflation, have eroded the profitability of manufacturing business in Britain – and to see how inflation accounting could be a useful step towards repairing some of the damage.

(c) *The effects of government prices and incomes policies on profitability*

We saw that wage-cost inflation pressures increased in Britain in the late 1960s. So it is not surprising to find that the recent period witnessed attempts by various governments to formulate and operate an effective incomes and prices policy.[2] First, there were the Labour Government's various measures of 1965–69; secondly, there was the period of unofficial restraint on prices and incomes from 1970–72 under the Conservative government; thirdly, there was the same government's statutory policy which lasted from 1972 to the early part of 1974. In principle, all prices and incomes policies have one central aim: to break the wage-cost and price spiral by establishing

---

[1] 2 July, 1977.

[2] Derek Lee, *Control of the Economy*, Heinemann Educational Books, 1974, p. 94.

machinery (which may be voluntary or statutory) to limit simultaneously the rate at which firms may increase their prices and worker groups their wages. In practice, however, the policies have invariably run into difficulties in dealing with various exceptional cases – for example, unavoidable import price increases; and the problem of larger-than-average wage claims from low-wage workers, and from those with rapidly increasing productivity. In the end, all the policies have been undermined by these (and other) factors, which have made it increasingly difficult to secure the continued co-operation of the firms and worker groups concerned.

It was significant that in 1974 a report by an influential House of Commons Committee recommended against the further use of prices and incomes policies as the main method of tackling Britain's inflation problem.

Although prices and incomes policies have not been very successful in their chief aim – overcoming inflation – they have from the viewpoint of business finance had a very considerable, and unfortunate, impact. For, in the main, these policies have been more effective in restricting rising prices than they have been in restraining incomes from employment. The result has been that company profits have, over the years, been continually and cumulatively squeezed.

The policies have also contained provisions designed to limit not only the level of company profits but also the amount of dividend which companies might distribute out of their profits. The idea behind this latter feature was that, in the common fight against inflation, shareholders should share in the sacrifices of the wage earners. This may have been good politics. But it was unsound economics, for enforced ploughbacks of profits by companies, via dividend restraint, would, other things being equal, tend to increase the market value of company securities. Thus shareholders would receive a capital appreciation to offset the dividends which they had foregone on account of dividend restraint. (By 1974 this point was becoming irrelevant, for many companies' profits were now so poor that they were no longer in a position to increase dividends.)

Special factors affecting company profitability and liquidity around 1974

(a) *Oil-deflation*

A special factor which affected business conditions was the rise in world oil prices which took place between 1973 and 1974. One effect of this increase was to reduce the effective annual purchasing power of consumers and businesses in the industrial countries as a whole by about $60,000 millions. Most governments in the industrial countries, faced with this new deflationary factor, were very wary about taking measures to restore domestic demand, when prices were already rising so fast. For the rise in oil prices, together with that of many other primary products, had put the balance of payments of several of the industrial countries into substantial deficit – and domestic reflation, when undertaken by any one country, might worsen its payments problem. Also there was the danger that reflating domestic demand might allow further scope for wage-cost inflation to express itself.

What therefore began to happen was that some of the industrial countries tried to find a way out of their difficulties by adopting policies – which included *deflationary* domestic measures – aimed at stimulating their exports and reducing their imports. Now it may be possible for an individual country to succeed in this. But it is clear that, since one country's exports are another country's imports, it is not possible for a large group of countries simultaneously to export themselves out of their combined recession and balance of payments difficulties. On the contrary, such beggar-my-neighbour policies would inevitably lead towards a multiple destruction of international trade and so increase the chances of a world depression.[1]

By the end of 1974 there were already signs (for example, rising unemployment in the major industrial countries) that this might already be happening. Not surprisingly the new threat to business prospects was reflected in widespread falls in Stock Exchange prices not only in London, but also in New York, Tokyo and other financial centres.

(b) *The British fuel crisis of early 1974*
A second factor which reinforced the downward trend in business prospects, and the fall in share prices, was Britain's 1974 fuel crisis. First, there was the disruption of Britain's oil supplies. At the end of 1973 the Arab oil-producing states reduced supplies of crude oil to most industrial countries, as part of their political pressure to achieve a settlement of the conflict with Israel. Since oil is a

---

[1] See Brinley Davies, *The U.K. and the World Monetary System*, Heinemann Educational Books, 1975, p. 89.

major source of power and raw materials, the cutback in oil supplies (though it turned out to be only a few per cent) resulted in some disruption of production in Britain and other industrial countries.

Secondly, in the winter of early 1974 there came the British coal miners' work to rule. This, in conjunction with the oil shortage, led the government to impose a three-day working week on industry with the aim of conserving power supplies. In the event the oil-producing states soon restored near-normal supplies to the west, while in Britain the coal miners' strike was quickly settled by the new Labour government, and a full working week resumed. Even so, the overall effect of the fuel crisis had been to put severe pressures on many companies' cash flows – 'liquidity' – and industrial production in Britain was still suffering from shortages of key components at the end of 1974. Moreover, the increase in world oil prices, from about $3 to $10 a barrel, through its effects on industrial costs, increased the pressures on companies' profitability and liquidity.

(c) *Monetary restraint and the 1974 financial crisis*

One result of the inflation in the early 1970s had been to convince a growing number of economists and politicians that a fast-rising supply of money, if not necessarily a prime cause of inflation, was certainly an important contributory factor. This change of attitude was reflected in the Bank of England's measures in 1974 to restrict the growth of the money supply. This monetary restraint, however valuable its contribution might be to Britain's long-term economic health, contributed further to the immediate deterioration in the financial and general business outlook.

One effect of the tighter money supply was to raise rates of interest, which made it more expensive for companies using short-term credit to finance current assets such as stocks of materials. Secondly, the new monetary climate made the clearing banks much more cautious about continuing to extend large amounts of credit to companies in difficulties, which might soon be forced into liquidation. This particularly applied to various insurance companies, property companies and fringe banks, whose operations had been badly hit by the falling prices of securities and property. Since this was a very important turn of events, it is worth examining in some more detail. The root of the matter lay in the very large monetary expansion which had taken place under the Conservative government in 1971–73. Since industrial investment continued – in spite of the apparently good expansion prospects – to run at a low level, a good part of the increased funds available through the banking system was lent to firms dealing in property. In the speculative atmosphere which then set in, the values of property were driven to very high levels which often bore little relation to their likely future rent-income. It was estimated[1] that by the end of 1974 the banking system had already advanced £2,776 millions to property companies. Then, in 1974, came the monetary restraint which cut off the flow of funds, reversed the speculation and took the bottom out of the property boom. The other factor making for falling property values was the introduction of a rent freeze on commercial properties, which substantially reduced their income. The fringe banks, the finance houses, the accepting houses, as well as the clearing banks themselves were in their turn now affected by the threatened bankruptcies of property companies. Towards the end of 1974 the clearing banks decided to put a limit of £1,300 millions on any further money they were willing to put into forty or so fringe banks that now needed support on account of collapsing property values. Even so, an additional £500 millions would apparently be needed to cope with further withdrawal of deposits from the secondary banking system by worried customers. Another difficulty was that as the liquidity position of industrial firms became more tight, so the banks came under pressure to lend funds in that direction rather than leave them tied up in the suspect secondary banking/property sector.

One suggested solution was that the government should relax its commercial rent freeze, and so allow property incomes, and values, to recover. This was actually announced in December 1974. Unfortunately the earlier boom had forced property values so high that it was doubtful whether relaxing rent controls – or indeed any other measure, short of another money-printing spree – would restore property prices to their former levels. It is in fact difficult to resist the conclusion that there was a considerable element of irresponsibility in the readiness with which the banking system was prepared to make funds available on a huge scale for property ventures, some of which were frankly speculative. At the time of reckoning in 1974, it was even suggested that 'the rate of increase in the money supply over the next twelve months [1975] may ultimately be dictated less by broad economic considerations than by the need to stave off a seizure in the

---

[1] *The Times*, 13 December, 1974.

banking system, which might precipitate the economy further down the road to severe recession'.[1]

(d) *The mood of the City in 1974*

We have already noted how the prolonged fall in security prices in 1973–74 weakened the asset position of the unit and investment trusts, pension funds and insurance companies. As a result, the role of these institutions as regular and substantial net purchasers of company securities was greatly reduced. In the summer of 1974 there were rumours that some of the institutions were actually being forced to sell large lines of blue chip shares in well-known British companies in order to obtain the cash needed to run their businesses.

Secondly, the falling trend of security prices, together with the low volume of dealings on an anxious stock market, greatly reduced the earnings on the Stock Exchange of jobbers and brokers. Several of these firms went bankrupt, and others were forced to merge, and lay off staff, in order to cut their expenses. This, in conjunction with the difficulties of the financial institutions, the property companies and the fringe banks, helped to generate an atmosphere of extreme pessimism in the City.

In fact, the dark mood of the City in 1974 attracted a considerable amount of criticism. There was by now little doubt that a recession was developing in Britain (and other industrial countries) as more and more firms began to reduce their output and their demand for labour. What was being argued however by some economists was that the London stock market dealers and institutional investors were, due to their position at the heart of the unsettled financial scene, greatly exaggerating the problems of the British economy as a whole. It was feared that the pessimism of the London financial community, as expressed in the astonishingly low level of share prices (and high historic market yields), would spread to the general business community and increase the risk that companies would undertake major cuts in investment spending, and so provoke a really severe depression. The following newspaper article is a good example of such criticism:

> Mr Wilson and Mr Heath have this in common: each in his day has become disenchanted with the City of London. Both have learnt to mistrust its collective judgement . . .

---

[1] *The Times*, 13 December, 1974.

For rumour, poor political information and poor political understanding, wrong inferences, weak reasoning and erratic decisions, the City as exemplified by the Stock Exchange, would be hard to beat at present. Alarmist and panicky at worst, at best prone to melancholy, there is nothing to touch it as a source of depression, dismay and disquiet. A great financial community, with a matchless history of achievement, is visibly losing its corporate nerve – and could unnerve the country, unless it pulls itself together . . . from current share prices, so pessimistically written down, you might suppose that British industry was on its knees. But this is not true. The values placed by a handwringing City on some of our finest manufacturing companies are seen to be grotesque, even offensive, when you consider their commercial record, their assets, resources, performance and potential. . . .

There are many who think that by its recent behaviour the City – more explicitly the Stock Exchange – is in danger of becoming a national millstone. They find the defeatism to which it has lately surrendered not only disappointing but pitiful. This is not to suggest that the City has nothing to worry about. Of course it has – shaky fringe banks, property speculators and other lame ducks. More will go under – the ones that were unsound in their beginnings. They were formed to make money for their founders, not to make anything else or provide some socially useful service. They belong to Mr Wilson's 'casino society'.

Our important manufacturing industries are totally distinct from the world of the sharp money man, the juggler interested in nothing but quick overnight profits. They are not distinct from the good elements in the City, however, but are on the contrary closely linked to them. Except in phases of abnormality (like the present), the City as an institution is industry's natural collaborator, both as patron and partner, supporting what is already established and worthwhile, financing the gifted newcomer or promising innovation. Much of the City is not trying just now.[1]

Was the unprecedented fall in share prices, and the City's pessimism, a panic reaction to what was merely a temporary slowdown in economic growth? Or was it an accurate early warning of a really severe recession? Readers of this book, looking back towards 1974 will be able to judge the answer for themselves!

Background to the November 1974 Budget
The final point which we shall consider is the political and policy response to the grave business situation around 1974. By the end of

---

[1] *The Times,* 24 August, 1974.

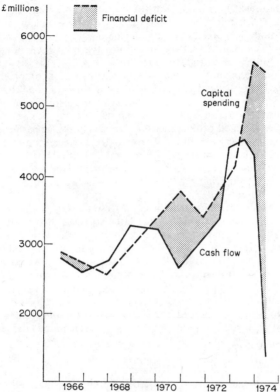

THE LONDON STOCK MARKET IN THE 1970s

£ millions

Financial deficit

6000

Capital spending

5000

4000

3000

Cash flow

2000

1966   1968   1970   1972   1974

Fig. 7.4. Company cash flow and capital spending.
Source: *Bank of England Quarterly Bulletin*, Dec. 1974.

1974 matters were clearly coming to a head, and on the financial front severe cash difficulties had now forced many companies into an excessive reliance on expensive short-term borrowing from the banks. A number of financial companies had already been forced to the wall and others were being supported by wide-scale rescue finance from the banking system – with the result that the banks themselves were suffering a loss of confidence. For example, the National Westminster Bank took the step of publicly denying rumours that it was having to ask for help from the Bank of England.

The *Bank of England Quarterly Bulletin* summed up the elements in the tight financial situation:

The situation has resulted from the impact of inflation on corporate finances, and it might have been recognized more widely and earlier had accounting practices generally been adapted to take account of inflation. The elements of the situation have both been building up, and seem likely to persist, for some time.

The long-term and fundamental problem is lack of profitability, particularly the lack of an adequate real return on capital invested; the immediate and acute manifestation of the problem in 1974 has been the rapid loss of liquidity, which had already been depleted by insufficient retained profits, measured in real terms, in earlier periods. The situation has been made worse by the financial strain of short-time working earlier in the year, and by the working of the price code; and it has been brought to a head by the much sharper rise in the cost of materials, requiring vastly increased sums to finance stocks and working capital.

As a result of inadequate internal resources, firms have heavily increased their borrowing over the last two years. Before the Budget many firms were increasingly being forced to the view that further additions to debt could not prudently be contemplated, and that, for them to survive, all avoidable expenditures would have to be eliminated. This has shown up a rapid pruning of investment plans, and would no doubt have resulted in widespread cutbacks in output, stocks, and employment. The efforts of firms individually to economise could only have worsened their collective situation, and a further tightening of trade credit might have exaggerated the financial stringency.[1]

The November 1974 Budget Measures

It was against this sombre background that the Chancellor of the Exchequer, Denis Healey, introduced in his November 1974 Budget a new set of economic measures, following on from those in his July and March Budgets. If these measures failed to take account of, and repair, the ill-fortunes of the company sector, the risk of further cutbacks in company investment and production and a further deepening of the recession would be very high.

As it turned out, Healey's Budget measures were, from a business point of view, not as bad as some commentators had feared they would be. First, the Chancellor accepted that inflation had falsely overstated many companies' profits and tax bills. Accordingly the Budget now provided for temporary corporation tax relief (worth in

---

[1] *Bank of England Quarterly Bulletin*, December 1974.

total about £775 millions) on increases in stock valuations above 10 per cent of trading profit for firms with closing stocks of £25,000 and over. (This must be compared, though, with the extra £495 millions which had earlier been levied in the form of increased advance corporation tax on companies in Healey's March 1974 Budget). The Chancellor also promised to continue some form of tax relief on stock appreciation in future years along the lines, it was assumed, of the forthcoming Sandilands Committee Report[1] on inflation accounting. One snag with these measures, however, was that some companies' profits, and therefore tax liabilities, were by now so small that they were not able to benefit fully from the new relief arrangements! It was, for example, estimated[2] that although British Leyland would now be entitled to £14 millions of relief its actual tax bill was currently only £5·5 millions. Another feature of the November Budget was that it provided for an increased initial tax allowance, from 40 per cent to 50 per cent, on expenditure on industrial building; plus a 100 per cent allowance for heat-insulation of existing buildings.

Secondly, the Budget, by relaxing somewhat the existing controls on company prices, aimed to bring in companies about £800 millions extra sales revenue, equivalent to about 1 per cent on the retail price index. (This was on the assumption – probably justified – that consumers would continue to buy goods at these higher prices.)

A third feature of the November 1974 Budget which was significant from the company point of view, was the proposed setting up of a semi-official City investment bank to lend medium-term capital to industry. It was hoped that in this way finance would be available for investment-led recovery from Britain's recession. The investment bank was to be set up through the Industrial and Commercial Finance Corporation (ICFC) (see p. 32), the main operating subsidiary of Finance for Industry (FFI), a medium-term credit institution owned by the commercial banks and the Bank of England. Under the new arrangement, the banks and institutions would lend up to £1,000 millions to the FFI, which would in turn be able to lend long-term to industry and so fill the gap caused by the ill-effects of the stock market crash on the London capital market. To encourage and help the banks to participate in the new scheme the Chancellor announced that their special deposits lodged at the Bank of England

---

[1] Published September 1975.
[2] *The Economist*, 16 November 1974, p. 91.

(then running at £900 millions) would now receive interest at the Treasury Bill rate of 11 per cent. One doubt however was whether the financial institutions – especially the pension funds, with their obligations to their trustees – would be prepared to tie up sufficient of their funds in what was effectively government paper, for long periods. Furthermore there was the question whether companies would, with their thin profits, be able to afford to borrow at high current interest rates from the FFI in order to finance their expansion. No doubt such finance was preferable to *ad hoc* credit from the banking system. But it was no substitute for an economic climate in which companies could earn healthy profits and finance their own expansion from retained earnings or from issues of debentures and shares on the open capital market.

Taking the 1974 November Budget as a whole there was a further and more fundamental question mark.[1] The November Budget was designed in essence to shift about 2 per cent of the country's gross national product into company profits and thence, it was hoped, into increased investment. The question was, where would these resources come from? For Government spending, according to the Budget, was actually planned to increase in real terms by $2\frac{3}{4}$ per cent annual, for the next four years. Equally, no release of resources could be looked for from the viewpoint of the balance of payments: on the contrary, more resources would need to be moved into improving Britain's foreign payments. So the only other main source was reduced consumption. Now the effect of the Budget and its related measures would be to add about 3 to 4 per cent to the retail price index, which (other things remaining equal) would reduce real consumption by a corresponding amount. However, if in the outcome, the higher prices resulting from the budget led to increased wage claims, the squeeze on consumption would clearly fail. This brings us to the key weakness of the November 1974 Budget, namely the absence of any effective accompanying incomes policy. Under the government's social contract – even assuming it was adhered to – worker groups were expecting to push up their wages *in line with increases in the cost of living*. In the words of *The Economist*[2]

> At its simplest, no strategy which involves shifting resources from consumer spending to exports and investment can work unless it

---

[1] *The Economist*, 16 November 1974, p. 85.
[2] 16 November, 1974.

contains some mechanism for ensuring that resources will be released. Until the British economy starts growing again with an incomes policy which ensures that wage earners do not pre-empt all the new resources, the only effect that a shuffling of financial resources can have is to accelerate the rate of inflation. And this, ultimately, must burn itself out in mass unemployment.

Sunrise – or a false dawn?

On 6 January, 1975, the FT index had fallen to 146. Some investors thought that the index might fall yet further; other investors believed that it would probably now bump along the bottom for the rest of the year. What actually took place was the most remarkable rise in share values ever witnessed on the London stock market, for within three weeks the FT share index had reached 252·3 – a rise of 73 per cent. The climb continued and by mid-March 1975 the FT share index had apparently stabilized around the 300 mark; by June it had reached 350.

What were the reasons for this unexpected change in the stock market? One factor was technical: the big institutional investors had held off buying for a considerable time and the more successful ones which had weathered the financial storm now had huge liquid funds – amounting to £3,500 millions – awaiting reinvestment. When some of these funds hit a thin stock market, share prices were bound to rise strongly. However, the new share boom was more than a temporary technical recovery: it seemed to have a life of its own, for turnover on the market remained at a high level as more and more investors got back into shares. Moreover the New York stock market was also rising steadily. And it is this which gives us the key to the new situation, which began at the time when the United States President announced new economic measures against the recession there, involving higher government spending and increased money supply and lower rates of interest. Soon the Bank of England too was able to reduce its minimum lending rate in stages and this was followed by cuts in the commercial banks' lending rates. The *Economist*[1] summed up the new situation:

> Stock markets across the world have turned round because politicians across the world have turned round, and are now more intent on fighting unemployment than inflation. They are replacing their

[1] 1 February, 1975, p. 13.

increases of taxes last autumn with cuts in the same taxes today, while central banks strive to send already negative real interest rates lower still. In nominally socialist countries like Britain the present stage of the trade cycle brings another bull point. Governments want to get out of this stage of recession by boosting industrial investment rather than consumption, and these make them more anxious not to antagonize industrialists.

However, the pessimists – who were still expecting share prices to fall back again – could point to the fact that the world was still slipping deeper into recession, while in Britain, with the prospect of continuing wage-cost inflation, the outlook for company profits remained poor, with more bankruptcies likely. Moreover the apparent improvement in Britain's export figures was largely spurious, being due to higher prices rather than increased volume.

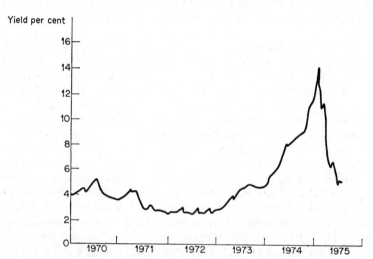

Fig. 7.5. Dividend yield on ordinary shares, 1970–1975.
Source: *The Economist*, 1 March, 1975.

Whether or not the share recovery was permanent, one thing quickly became clear – the London capital market had come back to life. As market yields now fell, more and more capital-hungry companies went on to the market for funds. In the three weeks up to mid-March 1975, a flood of rights issues took no less than £180 millions off the market, and it was estimated[1] that another £1,000 millions of rights issues would soon be on flow, covering the whole spectrum of private business from packaged bread to North Sea oil.

The stock market in the later 1970s

Total new company issues (mainly in the form of 'rights') amounted to nearly £1,600 million in 1975 – ten times the level of 1974, the year of the stock market crash. It should be noted that only a minor part of this sum was used for fixed investments. Most was raised with the tactical purpose of reducing the over-gearing (see p. 24) which had often arisen from companies' dependence upon bank-borrowing to finance stock appreciation (p. 93) in a time of rapid inflation. Rights issues in 1976 and 1977 relieved over-gearing further, so that new issues in 1978 were increasingly being used for companies' expansion programmes.

In 1976 the depressed state of the economy was reflected in a reduction of new company issues to £1,160 million. Slack conditions on the new issue market carried over into 1977 but later in that year a burst of new issue activity developed. An important factor was a stronger stock market reflecting better economic prospects in Britain. The FT ordinary share index started the year at 350, reached 500 in September and held 450 for the rest of 1977. The liquidity of the big institutional investors was now improving so that they were able to accommodate the demand for new issues at a time of attractively low dividend yields. As the *Midland Bank Review* put it[2]:

Expanding capital expenditure programmes were responsible for some of the fund-raising, whilst a sharp rise in commodity prices prompted others. A number of companies were influenced by the fact that a rights issue enabled them to increase their dividend by more than the statutory 10 per cent per annum. Several came forward with their second issue inside two years because they had not been able to raise all they had wanted at the first attempt (it is hard for a company to raise much more than about a fifth of its existing equity capitalization even though its requirements may be greater). However, the majority of decisions to tap the market were undoubtedly inspired by the desire to take advantage of opportunities that might not last.

---

[1] *Sunday Telegraph*, 16 March, 1975.
[2] *Midland Bank Review*, Spring 1978, p. 23.

Although the balance between their equity and loan capital was satisfactory, their liquidity was improved and they had no immediate use for the extra cash, many companies felt they should raise new funds while the conditions were favourable. It was the case of a buoyant stock market continuing to drag out issues. Remembering vividly the traumas of 1974, companies were taking the money while it was there as an insurance against being caught short in the future.

The failure of new flotations

We have indicated that the recovery of company issues after 1974 was based largely on rights issues of equity. But what of new flotations for companies coming on to the stock exchange for the first time for a listing of their shares? Their experience was an unhappy one, for few such issues were well-subscribed and issuing houses came to adopt a cautious attitude to them at a time when, on the face of it, stock market conditions were ideal for new flotations. One difficulty was that the criteria for new flotations are strict and that the costs of 'going public' may amount to around 10 per cent of the funds raised. The main factor, though, was apparently the reluctance of the institutional investors to provide high-risk funds for new companies. The smaller private investors, who are traditionally more inclined to take risks, were largely absent from the market, partly on account of the tax-erosion of investment funds.[1]

The failure of new flotations led to considerable concern in the City, not least on the stock exchange which, as a measure to help new companies, in September 1977 reduced from 35 per cent to 25 per cent the proportion of a company's equity which must be made available to the public. Perhaps a really sustained bull stock market would have attracted enough funds from institutional and private investors to float off new companies successfully. But there was little sign of that.

---

[1] *Midland Bank Review*, Ibid.

APPENDIX A: PREFERENCE SHARES

A preference share, like a debenture, carries a fixed rate of return on its nominal value. However, unlike debenture interest, the dividend on a preference share is not a *legal* claim on a company's earnings – it is paid only if the management decides that the company's profits are sufficient to allow this. Preference shareholders are however partly protected by the fact that no ordinary dividend may be declared unless the preference dividends have been paid in full. A second point to note is that preference shareholders have no legal claim for the repayment of their capital out of the company's assets if it should go into liquidation – though here again they do rank ahead of the company's ordinary shareholders.

Thus a preference shareholder has some, but by no means all, of the security of a debenture holder and bears some, but not all, of the risks of the ordinary shareholder. In a sense therefore a preference share is a halfway house between debentures and ordinary shares. Preference shares generally carry no say in the running of a company. This is because their dividends, as a prior claim, are less dependent upon profit performance than are those on ordinary shares. A company's preference shares may be divided into a number of classes each with its own priority ranking. Thus it might for example be stated in the company's provisions that the 1963 7 per cent preference dividend must be paid in full before the 1972 11 per cent preference dividend is paid. Alternatively some or all of the classes of preference share capital may rank *pari passu* – that is, equally with one another – as a claim on the company's profits.

Cumulative preference shares
A company which goes through a period of lean profits may decide to suspend dividends on its preference share capital. As a protection in this eventuality some preference shares are made *cumulative*; which means that if in a particular year low profits prevent the payment of the full rate of preference dividend, the deficiency must be met out of the profits of subsequent years before the ordinary shares can receive anything. In the case of *non-cumulative* preference shares if the divi-

dend is passed in any one year it is lost for good, no matter how much the company's profits may improve later. Nowadays most preference shares are cumulative – in fact unless the company's provisions relating to the issue state otherwise, preference shares are assumed to be cumulative.

Participating preference rights

A *participating* preference share allows the holder not only a fixed preference dividend, but also the right in certain circumstances to participate in the remaining profits of the company. Thus a company's provisions might allow that when the ordinary dividend rate exceeds 25 per cent, preference share holders may, over and above their (say) 7 per cent dividend, participate equally with the ordinary shareholders in any remaining profits up to a given maximum preference dividend – for example, 16 per cent. Some companies also issue what are called *preferential shares* and *preferential ordinary shares*; for practical purposes these can be regarded as similar to preference shares.

Convertible preference shares

It will be seen that a preference share is in some respects merely an inferior substitute for debentures. For when a firm's earnings are disappointing the preference shareholder shares in the risk of the equity holders. Yet when earnings are high the preference shareholder has no compensating advantage, since his dividend is normally at a fixed rate. So it is not surprising that preference shares have over the years fallen out of favour among the investing public. The trend away from preference shares was reinforced by the introduction in 1965 of corporation tax, which gave a distinct tax advantage to debenture finance (see p. 122). On the other hand debenture capital does, from a company's point of view, suffer from the fact that interest on it must be paid however bad its trading position may be. Whereas dividends on preference share capital need not be paid in years when earnings are low. In recent years some companies have adopted the practice of sweetening preference shares by including a *convertibility* provision. This allows preference shareholders the right to transfer into the company's ordinary shares within a certain time period, and thus share in its profits' growth. Should profits prove disappointing however they can retain their preference shares and the rather better security which they carry.

APPENDIX B: MEASURING A SHARE'S PERFORMANCE

(1) *Dividend rate*

Suppose a company has an ordinary share capital of £500,000, divided into shares of nominal value of 50 pence each. If it declares a dividend of £80,000, the dividend per share is thus 8 pence and the *rate of dividend* is therefore

$$\frac{8p}{50p} \times 100 = 16\%$$

this being the rate of return which a shareholder is getting, *expressed as a return on the nominal value* at which the shares were originally issued.

(2) *Dividend yield*

Suppose, on account of the satisfactory dividend, the share cited above becomes much sought after by investors. The consequence would then be that its 'second-hand' price on the Stock Exchange would rise – say, to 80 pence. If the company continues to declare an 8 pence dividend, an investor would be receiving *on the basis of the share's market price* a *dividend yield* of

$$\frac{16\% \times 50p}{80p} = 10\%$$

(3) *Earnings yield*

A share's dividend yield may in some circumstances be misleading. For example, a company with falling profits might still be prepared for a time to pay out of its reduced profits an unchanged dividend to the shareholders. Provided the share price remained unchanged the dividend yield would not reflect the company's changed fortunes, and would in fact overstate the share's prospects. *The earnings yield* of a share attempts to overcome this difficulty by basing its yield on the underlying earnings (profit) behind it by means of the formula

$$\frac{\text{net earnings (profit) per share}}{\text{market price}} \times 100$$

Suppose in the example above the £80,000 dividend was being paid out of a company profit of £240,000, which then fell to £120,000. Then the initial earnings yield would be

$$\frac{24p}{80p} \times 100 = 30\%$$

Subsequently (assuming that the share's market price was unchanged) the lower profit would be reflected in a reduced earnings yield:

$$\frac{12p}{80p} \times 100 = 15\%$$

(4) *The price-earnings ratio*
In the example above the earnings yield for the first case worked out at 30 per cent. This meant that the share in question would after approximately three years have earned an amount of profit equal to its present market value. This relationship is called a share's *price-earnings ratio* and is calculated by the formula

$$\frac{\text{market price of share}}{\text{earnings (profit) per share}}$$

Thus in the second case above the price-earnings ratio would, other things being equal, have risen to 80/12 = (nearly) 7 years.

Since the earnings yield and the price-earnings ratio both relate to the earnings position of a company it is clear that the two measurements must be connected. In fact, mathematically they are the reciprocal of each other. Thus in our example, when the earnings yield was 30 per cent the price-earnings ratio was about 3 (i.e. 100/30).

Price-earnings ratios have long been used as a yard-stick for share measurement in the United States. In recent years they have become much more widely adopted in Britain – which has made it easier to compare share performance in the two countries. It is also sometimes argued that the price-earnings ratio is a more logical concept than earnings yield, since the latter may seem to imply (wrongly) that the whole of a company's earnings are in practice available for distribution as dividends.

Summary to Appendix B

$$\text{Dividend rate} = \frac{\text{dividend per share}}{\text{nominal value}} \times 100$$

$$\text{Dividend yield} = \frac{\text{dividend rate} \times \text{nominal value of share}}{\text{market price of share}}$$

$$\text{Earnings yield} = \frac{\text{net profit per share}}{\text{market price}} \times 100$$

$$\text{Price-earnings ratio} = \frac{\text{market price of share}}{\text{net profit per share}}$$

APPENDIX C: A CASE STUDY: THE PERFORMANCE OF A SHARE

It was shown in Chapter 1 that an important indicator of a company's prospects is the trend of its earnings on capital employed together with the level of its assets. This is well illustrated in Rowlatt and Davenport's study[1] of Tesco's outstanding performance in the 1960s. The authors (who are themselves founders of a leading firm of investment counsellors) begin by presenting information obtained from Tesco's balance sheets for that period:

Table 8.1

Tesco Stores
£000's Indexes: 1962 = 100

Years to end February	Net trading assets	Index	Premises	Plant	Stocks	Net debtors
1961	5,100	73	2,879	1,058	2,215	−1,052
1962	6,949	100	4,002	1,804	2,778	−1,635
1963	8,290	119	4,921	2,404	3,281	−2,316
1964	9,297	134	5,827	2,711	4,385	−3,626
1965	11,970	172	8,156	3,704	5,595	−5,485
1966	15,411	222	11,007	6,294	7,239	−9,129
1967	18,726	270	13,528	7,257	9,282	−11,341
1968	23,019	332	16,599	8,651	11,149	−13,380

Source: Rowlatt and Davenport, op. cit., p. 77.

These figures refer to the four items used by a company in the course of its trading: premises and plant (net of depreciation), stock, and *net debtors* (that is, its debtors net of its creditors – what the authors call the current trading account). The net total of these four items constitute a company's *net trading assets*, which it uses to earn its income. It can be seen not only that Tesco's net trading assets trebled between 1961 and 1968 but that plant, premises and stocks grew even faster, this being made possible by the extremely large increase in net debtors. A feature of a well-managed supermarket is

---

[1] Op. cit., p. 76.

that while it receives normal trade of one month in which to settle
bills with its suppliers, it itself receives cash direct from its customers
and turns over its stocks in two or three weeks on average. Tesco
was able to exploit this feature, together with its ability as it expanded
its operations to obtain lower prices from bulk suppliers, so effectively
that from 1965 its stocks were actually greater than its net debtors –
in other words, Tesco's trading operations were now in effect being
financed by its own suppliers! The outcome of Tesco's able management in terms of profits and share dividends is to be seen on the next
set of figures, calculated by Rowlatt and Davenport from Tesco's
profit and loss accounts for that period:

Table 8.2

	Profit before tax and interest	Index	Profit as % NTA (previous year)	Earnings index	Dividend index
1961	1,219	86		80	81
1962	1,413	100	27·7	100	100
1963	1,699	120	24·4	117	133
1964	2,450	173	29·6	160	200
1965	3,576	253	38·5	191	238
1966	5,286	374	44·1	260	344
1967	6,669	472	43·3	300	372
1968	8,363	590	44·6	355	383

Source: Rowlatt and Davenport, op. cit., p. 77.

Rowlatt and Davenport then compare Tesco's excellent performance with that of one of its biggest retailing rivals, Allied
Suppliers (backed by the Unilever organization) which was basing its
expansion plans on a mixture of self-service and traditional sales
outlets:

Table 8.3

Allied Suppliers and Tesco
£000's; Index: 1962 = 100
(Years to January 1st and March 1st respectively)

| | Allied Suppliers | | Tesco | |
| | Net trading assets | | Net trading assets | |
	Actual	Index	Actual	Index
1961	37,767	87	5,100	73
1962	43,612	100	6,949	100
1963	44,751	103	8,290	119
1964	45,850	105	9,297	134
1965	47,500	109	11,970	172
	Stocks	Net debtors	Stocks	Net debtors
1961	18,517	−7,292	2,215	−1,052
1962	20,953	−8,055	2,778	−1,635
1963	22,460	−11,359	3,281	−2,316
1964	23,278	−11,626	4,385	−3,626
1965	23,582	−11,191	5,595	−5,485

| | Profits before interest and tax | | | Profits before interest and tax | | |
| | | | As % of NTA | | | As % of NpA |
	Actual	Index	(previous year)	Actual	Index	(previous year)
1961	4,267	86		1,219	86	
1962	4,968	100	13·2	1,413	100	27·7
1963	5,419	109	12·4	1,699	120	24·4
1964	5,783	116	12·9	2,450	173	29·6
1965	5,901	119	12·9	3,576	253	38·5

Source: Rowlatt and Davenport, op. cit., page 81.

As the authors put it:

Quite a perfunctory examination of its financial history would have shown [that Allied Suppliers] could not possibly be as good a growth investment as Tesco. . . . As the comparative figures for return on capital employed plainly indicate Allied was not using its resources nearly as effectively as Tesco [possibly on account of its smaller outlets and inadequate stock control].[1]

Finally Rowlatt and Davenport compare the performance of Tesco and Victor Value. Again, Victor Value could not match Tesco's efficient expansion and in 1968 it was bought out by Tesco at a cost of only 4 per cent of the latter's share capital.

[1] Op. cit., p. 80.

Table 8.4

Victor Value
£000's; Indexes: 1962 = 100

Years to December 31st	Net trading assets	Index	Premises	Plant	Stocks	Net debtors
1960	1,243	47	586	660	955	−958
1961	2,212	84	1,066	1,223	1,522	−1,599
1962	2,636	100	1,289	1,392	1,738	−1,783
1963	3,373	128	1,292	1,755	2,342	−2,016
1964	3,529	134	1,703	1,883	2,248	−2,305
1965	3,611	137	1,990	2,278	2,272	−2,929
1966	4,849	191	3,052	3,425	2,841	−4,469

	Profit before tax and interest	Index	Profit as % NTA (previous year)	Earnings index	Dividend index
1960	528	78		87	64
1962	619	91	49·8	100	80
1962	678	100	30·7	100	100
1963	684	101	25·9	117	120
1964	764	113	22·7	120	132
1965	705	104	20·0	122	132
1966	548	81	15·2	74	132

Source: Rowlatt and Davenport, op cit., page 82.

The authors are careful to remind us, however, that there are limitations to this approach:

For one thing, the asset values of supermarkets are exceptionally amenable to this sort of treatment. Their premises and plant are usually well sited in good shopping areas, and their stocks – all of them goods for sale – are worth, by and large, what they say they are. One cannot always assume as much with the asset value of old textile mills in Lancashire, and stock valuation in heavy engineering groups with long production cycles and huge ranges of spare parts, is notoriously arbitrary. As so often ... one must be prepared to do nine routine statistical assessments which end up meaning very little for every one that is significant and helpful. For all that, when a light does shine through the gloom of figures it can shine very brightly indeed.[1]

---

[1] Op. cit., p. 83.

APPENDIX D: TAXATION AND BUSINESS FINANCE

Capital gains taxation

Under the tax laws, anyone who makes a *capital gain* by selling chargeable assets at a price above that at which they were acquired is liable for tax on that gain. The term chargeable asset, as defined by the tax laws, includes company securities as well as most forms of property (with the exception of a person's main home, certain types of personal property, and savings certificates and life assured policies and annuities). Capital gains taxation in Britain has evolved in three stages:

(a) In 1962 a tax on *short-term* capital gains was introduced. This was charged at the same rate as personal income tax, and included capital gains on securities sold within twelve months of their acquisition (for land, the limit was three years).

(b) In 1965 capital gains taxation, at a flat rate of 30 per cent, was extended to cover *long-term* capital gains, including securities sold more than twelve months after acquisition.

(c) In April 1971 the short-term capital gains tax was abolished and replaced by the flat-rate long-term capital gains tax, which now came to apply to all capital gains. At present (1975), the rate of capital gains tax is 30 per cent.

Investors are allowed for tax purposes to set off any capital losses which they may make against their gains; when not fully used up in one year, any remaining capital losses may be off-set against capital gains in subsequent years. Individuals who make capital gains on relatively small sales of securities – at present a maximum annual total of £500 – are exempt from capital gains tax. Long-term capital gains on sales of government securities are exempt from tax; since 1969 however short-term gains on government securities have been taxable.

It is not within the scope of this book to analyse all the implications of capital gains taxation.[1] It is necessary, though, to look at

---

[1] See, for example, C. T. Sandford, *Realistic Tax Reform*, Charles Knight, 1971.

some adverse effects which it may have had on the raising of share capital:

(a) A capital gains tax may, by reducing the rewards to investors, impair the supply of share capital available to companies – particularly in the more risky areas of business enterprise, where the successful investor generally hopes to receive his financial reward in the form of rapid capital growth.

(b) When there is inflation, what appear to be capital gains are often illusory – and may be actual losses. For example, if the market price of some shares sold by an investor has risen 15 per cent over a period when the general level of prices has increased by, say, 50 per cent, the real value of the shares will actually have fallen, resulting in an effective capital loss. Nevertheless the investor in question will still be required to pay tax on his capital gain. In these circumstances the anomalous effect of the capital gains tax could well deter investment in shares.

(c) The capital gains tax has up to the present only been applied to realized capital gains. Thus provided the investor does not sell securities, he pays no tax. There is therefore a risk that investors will, when share prices are rising, try to defer selling them as much as possible, with the result that dealings on the Stock Exchange become thinner, and fluctuations in share prices greater.

(d) Since transactions in government securities are exempt from long-term capital gains, the relative attraction to investors of holding company shares is reduced, and there is a tendency for financial resources to be re-directed away from companies and into the government sector.

(e) In some circumstances[1] it may pay investors to reduce their total liability for capital gains by selling some of their weaker shares at a loss towards the end of the tax year. This can result in unsettling falls in the market prices of these shares, and damage not only the prospects of other investors but also the financial standing of the companies concerned.

(f) Most investors find it difficult to assess their liability for capital gains taxation, and not uncommonly find it necessary to employ the services of professional tax advisers. This inconvenience factor may also deter investment in company securities.

Taking all these points into consideration it seems likely that, however well-advised its introduction may have been from a general

---

[1] See R. J. Briston, op. cit., p. 437.

fiscal point of view, the effect of capital gains tax on business finance has probably been adverse.

The taxation of company profits

A company's profits are in principle, as income, liable to taxation. Up to 1964 companies in Britain were taxed on a two-tier basis. First, they were liable for *profits tax* at a rate of 15 per cent of their total *net profit* (that is, after deducting expenses, depreciation allowances and interest payments on debenture and other loan capital). Secondly, they were liable to *income tax* at the *standard rate* (41·25 per cent, in 1964) on their total profits, net of expenses and depreciation allowances (but not interest payments). The total rate of taxation on company profits in 1964 was thus around 56 per cent. Dividends received by company shareholders who were paying income tax at the standard rate were not liable for any further tax, since the company in question was regarded as having already paid it at source on their behalf. Shareholders who were liable to income tax at less than the standard rate were allowed to claim a tax rebate from the tax authorities while shareholders on high rates of income tax were required to make a further tax payment in respect of their additional tax liabilities on their dividends. This feature reflected an attempt to incorporate an element of equity into company taxation, inasmuch as richer shareholders were required to pay a higher rate of tax on (distributed) company profits than less well-off shareholders.

In 1965 a new system of company taxation was introduced, which abandoned the former link between profits tax and company income tax, in order to aim at new objectives (see below). Under the terms of the 1965 Finance Act income tax on company profits was abolished while the profits tax was increased to 40 per cent and now became known as *corporation tax*. As far as profits retained by companies were concerned, that was the end of the story. In the case of profits distributed as dividends, however, shareholders were further liable to income tax according to their personal income rate. (For administrative convenience this was actually deducted at source at the standard rate by the company, the shareholder in question then paying or claiming the necessary tax adjustment.)

Corporation tax and profit retentions

One aim of corporation tax was to encourage companies to retain, and invest, a higher proportion of their profits: for whereas retained profits bore only corporation tax, distributed profits were subject both to corporation tax and to personal income tax by shareholders. Hence the lower the proportion of profits distributed by a company the less would be the combined tax paid in profits. This can be seen by taking the hypothetical case of a company which had formerly been distributing the whole of its (post-tax) profits. The effect on it of introducing corporation tax, per £100 of profit, is shown in table 8.5. It will be seen that the result is a substantial fall in the profit available for distribution.

Table 8.5 The effect of corporation tax on a company distributing all its profit.

	Old System	
	£	£
Profit		100·00
Profits tax	15·00	
Income tax	41·25	
		56·25
Net dividend		43·75
	New System	
Profit		100·00
Corporation tax		40·00
		60·00
Income tax		24·75
Net dividend		35·25

A company which had formerly distributed only one-half of its post-tax profit would be able under the new system, as table 8.6 shows, to increase both its dividend and its retained earnings. The higher the company's rate of retention of profit, the more favourable its tax position would become.

On 1 April, 1973 a modification of corporation tax took effect, one aim of which was to end tax discrimination in favour of retained profits. Under the new *imputation system*, companies became liable for an increased rate of corporation tax on their total profits. This was however offset by the fact that part of the increase was to be passed (imputed) to the shareholders in the form of a tax credit. According to the *Investor's Chronicle*,[1]

---

[1] *Beginners Please*, Associated Book Publishers, 1973, p. 204.

the new imputation system will be more favourable with regard to distributed profits than its predecessor and the general effect will be to lessen the collective tax burden of the company and its shareholders, taken together, at the expense of a heavier tax bill on the retained profit.

On the other hand it

will be advantageous to companies which make capital gains and wish to retain these in the company and in such cases will, to a certain extent, compensate for the heavier taxation on retained profits[1].

Table 8.6   The effect of corporation tax on a company distributing half its profit

Old System

	£	£
Profit		100·00
Profits tax	15·00	
Income tax	41·25	
		56·25
Available for dividend		43·750
Retained		21·875
Net dividend		21·875

New System

	£
Profit	100·00
Corporation tax	40·00
Available for dividend	60·00
Retained	21·875
Gross dividend	38·125
Income tax	15·726
Net dividend	22·399

Whether the introduction of corporation tax actually had much effect in increasing companies' investments is doubtful: 'A survey of company results suggests that the vast majority of companies retained dividends where possible regardless of the level of retention'.[2] Even in those cases where companies did retain more of their profits, this might merely take the form of increased paper assets, rather

[1] Ibid.

[2] R. J. Briston, op. cit., p. 448.

than real investment in physical assets. Also, increased investment out of higher retained profit would where it occurred tend to be at the expense of other companies seeking new finance from the now reduced resources of the shareholding public. Further, there is also the more general doubt of whether companies investing out of retained profits do so as efficiently as those which have had to face the discipline of using the open capital market. Taking into account these factors then it seems doubtful whether this aim of the 1965 system of company taxation was very successful, or even well-advised. It is significant that in West Germany since the War it has been government policy to encourage the *distribution* of company profits, by taxing dividends at a much *lower* rate than retained earnings.

An unwanted effect of corporation tax was that it reduced the value to companies of the taxation allowance on the depreciation of their taxed assets – it can be calculated that since corporation tax was 40 per cent compared with the former combined profits tax and income tax of 56 per cent, this would effectively fall from 73 per cent to 52 per cent. It was partly to counter this effect, that the government introduced, in 1966, a system of *investment grants*, in the form of immediate cash payments to businesses purchasing new equipment (see p. 127).

Corporation tax and overseas investment

A second aim of corporation tax was to discourage companies in Britain from investing overseas – a reflection of the country's perennial balance of payments difficulties. Under the double taxation arrangements which Britain has with many other countries, companies in Britain are allowed to set the tax which they have paid on profits abroad against their British tax liabilities. Before 1965 this meant that they could write off 56 per cent of any foreign profits tax free (this being the combined profits plus income tax rate of British company taxation at that time). With the introduction of corporation tax, however, the domestic tax relief on the foreign profits of British companies became worth only 40 per cent – the going rate of corporation tax. As a result, many more companies operating in Britain would find themselves with an increased net tax liability on foreign profits. It was intended that this would make companies think twice about undertaking new foreign investments, as well as encouraging them to repatriate foreign profits back to Britain, where the company tax rate was now relatively low.

Corporation tax and debenture finance

A third effect of corporation tax was to make it more expensive for companies to raise share capital, compared with debentures. Even before 1965 there was a tax bias in favour of debenture finance, inasmuch as debenture interest was allowable as a deduction from profits for tax purposes while dividends for shareholders were not. However, as the rate of profits tax was only 15 per cent, the tax differential in favour of loan finance was relatively small. Under the system of company taxation from 1965, however, interest on loan capital became allowable against corporation tax at a rate of 40 per cent (soon increased to 45 per cent and later, in 1974, to 52 per cent). The increased advantages of debenture finance are illustrated in the following table, showing the new tax position of a company with no

Table 8.7 The differential effect of corporation tax on loan-finance and share-finance

Company A

	£
Ordinary share capital	500,000
10% preference capital	500,000
Total capital employed	1,000,000
Profit .	100,000
Corporation tax	45,000
	55,000
Preference dividend	50,000
Available for ordinary	5,000

Company B

	£
Ordinary share capital	500,000
10% debenture capital	500,000
Total capital employed	1,000,000
Profit	100,000
Tax allowance on debenture interest	50,000
	50,000
Corporation tax	22,500
Available for ordinary	27,500

loan capital, compared with one having 50 per cent of its capital in loan form. Preference dividend and debenture interest are assumed to be 10 per cent and corporation tax 45 per cent (these being figures typical of the period of around 1970).

Not surprisingly, there was a tendency after 1965 for debentures to gain ground at the expense of preference shares:

Table 8.8   The decline in preference shares.

Percentage of total company issues

Year	Loan capital	Preference capital	Equity
1963	60·3	3·3	36·4
1964	56·6	2·6	40·8
1965	90·3	0·6	9·0
1966	75·1	2·6	22·3
1967	81·5	1·4	17·2
1968	45·8	0·5	53·8
1969	67·1	nil	32·9

Source: *Midland Bank Review*, February 1972

How much of this was due to the impact of corporation tax and how much to other factors is difficult, on this evidence alone, to say.

In the 1970s the role of preference capital remained small, while in a period of generally high and uncertain interest rates, the proportion of equity issues rose sharply at the expense of debenture finance.

Table 8.9   The decline in debentures.

Percentage of total issues

Year	Loan capital	Preference capital	Equity
1970	80·4	4·9	14·7
1971	51·3	1·9	46·8
1972	30·9	1·1	68·0
1973	20·4	6·7	73·0
1974	26·4	—	73·6
1975	13·5	2·8	83·7
1976	8·0	3·8	88·2
1977	9·9	3·6	86·5

Source: *Midland Bank Review,* Spring 1978.

Investment allowances and investment grants

The tax authorities allow a company to treat the funds which it sets aside to cover depreciation of its fixed assets as part of its costs; they are thus exempt from corporation tax. Unfortunately, when there is inflation, the tax-free depreciation allowances accumulated are unlikely to meet the full cost of replacing a company's fixed assets. The remainder of its replacement finance will thus have to come from its taxed profits (see p. 89). To help overcome this difficulty successive governments have introduced extra forms of depreciation assistance for companies. The first of these was called an *initial allowance*. It was introduced in 1945 and allowed companies to bunch their depreciation tax allowances into the early part of the life of fixed assets; they thus received, in effect, an interest-free government loan on their fixed investments. In 1954 a system of *investment allowances* was introduced which allowed companies to depreciate assets over their life-time by more than their original cost. It was calculated[1] that in the period 1962–65 the depreciation allowances received in total by firms amounted to nearly twice the actual rate of depreciation of their fixed capital assets.

In 1966 investment allowances were replaced by cash *investment grants* at a rate, first of 20 per cent, and later 25 per cent of the purchase cost of new fixed assets. One reason for the change was that the introduction of corporation tax had reduced the benefits of the old investment allowances. Secondly, the government believed cash grants would be a more attractive investment inducement. Thirdly, investment grants could be used 'in the national interest' to discriminate between different industries. Thus companies in high unemployment areas received a 40 per cent investment grant (later, 45 per cent), while service industries were excluded, and so remained under the investment allowance system.

A feature of cash grants is that they help efficient and inefficient companies alike; whereas tax allowances, being a charge against profits, only reduce the tax bill of profitable companies – those making no profit receive no tax benefit. In view of this, the government decided in 1970 to abolish investment grants, and replace them by investment allowances on the purchase of new and second-hand assets, at a rate of 60 per cent of cost in the first year, and 25 per cent of the written-down asset value in subsequent years.

---

[1] F. W. Paish, op. cit., p. 85.

APPENDIX E: THE ROLE OF THE NATIONAL ENTERPRISE BOARD

Introduction

In its 1975 Industry Bill the government proposed to set up a state *National Enterprise Board*. Under the immediate control of a business-man, Sir Don Ryder, the NEB is aimed to change the structure of the British economy.[1]

1. The NEB will be able to acquire share ownership in any leading company to the extent of £10 millions or a 30 per cent control. Acquisitions beyond these limits will require the consent of the Secretary of State for Industry. The NEB will have at its initial disposal £700 millions of public funds and will be expected to inject capital into key growth industries where investment levels have been too low. The NEB is also expected to aim for an 'adequate' return on its invested capital. Since its proposed funds of £700 millions are nevertheless small compared with the total scale of private industry's finances, the NEB will be expected to rely a good deal on persuasion in its attempts to increase the level of investment and rationalize the structure of private firms.

2. The Industry Bill suggests giving the Secretary of State, in consultation with the NEB, wide powers of intervention in private industry:

(a) He may acquire company assets through the NEB to stop a foreign take-over bid.

(b) He may direct the NEB to invest in leading companies with financial difficulties.

(c) He may request information from companies on their operations.

3. It is envisaged that, under the auspices of the NEB, leading companies will be prepared to undertake planning agreements with the government on their future expansion plans. Companies doing so will get NEB assistance and will, where eligible, be assured of continuing regional development grants.

4. The companies concerned will be required to disclose in advance decisions affecting output, productivity, sales and acquisitions of fixed

---

[1] *The Economist*, 8 February, 1975.

assets, take-overs, closures, etc. This information may be made available by the Secretary of State to the relevant trade unions. Thus an essential object of the NEB will be to promote communication and co-operation between firms and their employees.

How successful the NEB will be, remains to be seen. One danger is that it may dissipate its funds, and energies, in the support of inefficient lame duck firms. Another problem is whether a central body such as the NEB (or its defunct forerunner the Industrial Reorganization Corporation[1]) necessarily knows best how to restructure private industry. What is clear however is that the continued inability, or unwillingness, of many private firms to generate or raise capital on a really large scale, has naturally led to the prospect of growing state intervention in the ownership and control of business. To this extent the financial role of the City of London in general, and the small investor in particular, will inevitably diminish.

The National Enterprise Board in operation
After a controversial birth, the National Enterprise Board made in 1976, its first year of operation, a pre-tax profit of £51 millions representing a return of 11·8 per cent on its capital employed. The NEB was operating in four main areas.[2]
1. As a holding company for government shareholdings in (mainly 'lame-duck') industries. In 1976 the NEB provided £500 millions in this direction. In the machine-tool market, the old-established firm of Alfred Herbert was lent much-needed finance. The NEB changed Herbert's management, started a five-year rolling plan, arranged improved business and financial reporting and as a result saw a £13·4 million loss in 1975 turned round to a small profit in 1976. NEB's involvement in Ferranti followed a similar pattern. For Rolls Royce the NEB put up £38 millions of share capital and £17 millions of loans to support research and development in readiness for a recovery in the aero-engine market. NEB's involvement in British Leyland was more questionable. Huge sums of public money were injected, yet in 1978 there was still little prospect of British Leyland finding its feet.
2. The NEB was active in operations to up-date the structure of

---

[1] See Derek Lee, op. cit., p. 42.
[2] *The Economist*, 7 May, 1977, p. 76.

British industry, mainly in four sectors: industrial trucks; industrial diesel engines; office machinery; and electronics. In the last field, investments of £50 millions were being planned for 1978 in semi-conductors and associated soft-ware – industries which had been pioneered in Japan and the United States but in which several European countries, with government backing, were now undertaking heavy investment programmes.

3. The NEB assisted a number of firms to tender for 'know-how' contracts abroad. The firm of Allied Investments got £1 million of equity and £1½ millions of loan capital to help it secure export deals for planning, equipping and managing hospitals in the lucrative Middle East market.

4. The NEB helped a dozen small companies – mainly in technology – needing minority equity stakes of typically £½ million to further their expansion.

The National Enterprise Board's share investments have come out of government funds in the shape of 'public dividend capital'. When the NEB makes an adequate profit it plans to return at least 10 per cent back to the government annually. The NEB's loans to industry come out of borrowing from the government National Loan Fund, typically at around 13 per cent to 15 per cent in 1977.

The NEB's first year of operation was relatively free from major controversy. Advocates of a free capital market continued, however, to question its ability to rescue lame ducks (especially British Leyland) and to spot 'winners', and to criticize its alleged tendency to offer softer-than-commercial terms on its funds. The Industrial Reorganization Corporation, a forerunner of the NEB, was destroyed by a change of government. The NEB, by contrast, showed signs of co-existing successfully with capitalism and long surviving its controversial birth.

APPENDIX F: INFORMATION FOR USE IN INVESTMENT GAMES

Scale of brokers' commission charged on share deals
The total value of the share (or other security) which is being bought or sold is known as the *consideration*. The following simplified scale is recommended for use in investment games:

Consideration	Brokerage
Up to £5000	$1\frac{1}{2}\%$ with a minimum of £7
Next £5,000	$1\frac{1}{4}\%$
Over £10,000	1%

It should be noted that in practice

(a) there is a reducing scale of charges beyond a £15,000 consideration.
(b) value-added tax is now payable on brokerage. Thus the $1\frac{1}{2}$ per cent rates becomes in effect

$$1\frac{1}{2}\% \times \frac{108}{100} = 1.62\%.$$

Similarly the 1 per cent rates becomes 1·08 per cent and so on.

When a particular share is bought and sold *within the account*, the investor pays only one brokerage commission on the two transactions.

Contract stamp
This is a duty levied by the government on all sales and purchases of securities. It may be considered negligible and disregarded in investment games. The actual rates are:

Consideration	Contract stamp
Up to £100	nil
Exceeds £100 but not £500	10p
Exceeds £500 but not £1,500	30p
Exceeds £1,500	60p

Transfer stamp

This is another stamp duty levied by the government on the *purchase* of most shares. The nominal rate is 2 per cent of the consideration, and this figure may be used in investment games.

In practice, the *effective* rate of transfer stamp duty is often rather more than 2 per cent, on account of the fact that the scale is broken down into steps:

Consideration	Transfer stamp
Up to £5	10p
Exceeds £5 but not £100	20p for each £10
Exceeds £100 but not £300	40p for each £20
Exceeds £300	£1 for each £50

An explanation of key concepts used in the Financial Times Share Information Service

The information on the following thirteen companies' shares is taken from the *Financial Times* of Friday, 21 March, 1975:

1974/75 High	1974/75 Low	Stock	Price	+ or −	Div net	cover	Yield gross	P/E
53	20	Rolls-Royce Motors	43	−1	14	1·6	12·2	7·4
21¾	5½	Brit Leyland	9	......	2	—	8·3	—
82	15	Fidelity Radio 10 p	37xd	......	39·6	φ	16·0	φ
122	58	EMI 50p	91xr	−2	t12·5	3·1	10·5	6·4
135	59	Wedgwood	118xa	......	t20·4	6·0	6·4	6·6
59	5	Court Line	13⧣	......	19·7	1·4	56·5	1·8
355	143	Fisons £1	280	−3	†8·9	2·6	4·7	11·5
51	15	London Brick	37	−3	‡10	2·9	‡	5·0
49	23	Cedar Inv.	45	......	◆6·8	1·2	5·6	21·4
54	23	Austin (James)	44	......	b14	3·3	12·4	3·6
275	135	Br. Home Strs	269	−5	g28·2	2·5	3·9	16·8
46	7½	Rotaflex GB 10p	21	......	h7·2	5·6	5·1	4·9
68	21½	Unigate	41	−1	¶10·2	2·0	hn9·4	8·4

The meanings of the column headings are as follows:

1974/75 High Low. These two columns refer to the share's highest and lowest market price (in pence) for the time period in question.

Stock. This describes the security in question: in this case, ordinary shares. Unless otherwise stated the par value of shares is 25p.

Price. This column gives the share's price, in pence, at the end of the day's stock market trading.

+ or −. This shows how much the share's price has changed, in pence, over the day's trading.

Dividend net. This gives the company's dividend for the latest year, net of tax, and measured as a percentage of the share's par value.

Cover. This shows the number of times that the company's profits cover the amount paid out as dividend.

Yield, gross. This gives the dividend as a percentage yield on the share's market price. The term 'gross' means the dividend is taken before deduction of tax.

P/E. This refers to the share's price-earnings ratio – see p. 114.

It will be seen that in the case of Rolls-Royce all the columns contain appropriate entries. For British Leyland however the cover and P/E data are absent. This reflected the fact that although the company had earlier declared a dividend, it now seemed unlikely, on account of its current trading difficulties, that any further similar dividend would be declared – in which case the cover and P/E data would be indeterminate (or even non-existent).

Key to main symbols used in FT share information

xd. This stands for *ex dividend.* It means that a dividend recently declared, but not yet paid, belongs to the previous seller of the share, and not to whoever may have purchased the share when the dividend is actually paid; only future dividends will belong to the buyer of the share.

Normally the buyer of a share can expect that he will be entitled to any dividend paid on a share: we then say that the share is *cum dividend.* Unless a share is specifically quoted 'ex divi' it is assumed to be 'cum'.

Φ. This means that figures or a report are being awaited from the company in question.

xr. This stands for *ex rights.* It means that a previous holder of the share is entitled to 'rights' previously announced but not yet issued. Unless a share is specifically quoted 'ex rights' it is assumed to be 'cum'.

xc. (no example available on 21 March, 1975). This stands for *ex cap*: a previous holder would be entitled to a previously announced scrip issue.

xa. This stands for *ex-all,* meaning that all previous supplementary advantages – whether dividend, rights or scrip – are excluded for the new purchaser of the share in question.

t. Indicates that dividend and cover relate to previous dividend and the P/E ratio based on latest annual earnings.

$\#$. Price at time when dealings in the share were suspended.

†. An *interim dividend* has since been increased or resumed. An 'interim' means an early part-payment of the 'final' year dividend later announced by a company.

‡. An interim has since been reduced, passed or deferred.

♦. A merger bid or reorganization in progress.

b. Official estimate (based, for example, on company prospectus).

g. Assumed dividend and yield.

h. Assumed dividend and yield after scrip issue.

¶. Indicated dividend after impending scrip and/or rights issue: the cover quoted then refers to a previous dividend or forecast.

BIBLIOGRAPHY

Books

V. Anthony, *Banks and Markets*, Heinemann Educational Books, 1972

R. J. Briston, *The Stock Exchange and Investment Analysis*, George Allen & Unwin 2nd Ed., 1973

Gordon Cummings, *Investment*, Penguin, 1973

Brinley Davies, *The United Kingdom and the World Monetary System,* Heinemann Educational Books, 1975

T. G. Goff, *Theory and Practice of Investment*, Heinemann, 1971

J. Hacche, *Economics of Money and Income*, Heinemann Educational Books, 1971

Investors Chronicle, Beginners Please, Associated Book Publishers, 1973

J. M. Keynes, *The General Theory of Employment Interest and Money*, Macmillan, 1936

Derek Lee, *The Control of the Economy*, Heinemann Educational Books, 1974

A. J. Merrett, M. Howe, G. D. Newbould, *Equity Issues and the London Capital Market*, Longmans, 1967

F. W. Paish, *Business Finance*, Pitman 4th ed., 1968

M. S. Rix, *Investment Arithmetic*, Pitman, 3rd Ed., 1971

James Rowlatt and David Davenport, *Guide to Saving and Investment*, David & Charles, 1971

C. T. Sandford, *Realistic Tax Reform*, Charles Knight, 1971

Ajit Singh, *Take-overs Their Relevance to the Stock Market and the Theory of the Firm*, Cambridge University Press, 1971

Frank Vogl, *German Business after the Economic Miracle*, Macmillan, 1973

Articles

'An Analysis of Take-overs', W. B. Reddaway, *L.B.R.*, April 1972

'Developing a European Capital Market', John M. Weiner, *L.B.R.*, July 1967

'The Profitability of British and American Industry', A. J. Merrett and John Whittaker, *L.B.R.*, January 1967

'Inflation and Declining Profits', Colin Clark, *L.B.R.*, October 1974

'The Profits of British Industry', G. J. Burgess and A. J. Webb, *L.B.R.*, April 1974

'Profitability of British Manufacturing Industry', M. Panic and R. E. Close, *L.B.R.*, July 1973

'Investment: Art, Science or What?', Basil Taylor, *L.B.R.*, January 1969

'The Capital Gains Tax', Professor A. J. Merrett, *L.B.R.*, October 1965

'UK and the EEC: the Prospects for Finance', W. A. P. Manser, *N.W.B.R.*, February 1972

'The Small Business and the Economic Climate', Bernard Hollowood, *N.W.B.R.*, February 1970

'Special Arrangements for Financing Exports', *M.B.R.*, August 1972

'The Committee of Industry on Small Firms – Midland Bank's Evidence', *M.B.R.*, February 1970

'Taxation of Capital Gains in the United Kingdom – A General Survey', *M.B.R.*, February 1971

'European Capital Markets', *B.B.R.*, August 1971

'The Involvement of EEC Banks in Industry', *B.B.R.*, February 1974

'Investment in Britain', *B.B.R.*, November 1973

'Capital Finance for Industry', *B.B.R.*, November 1973

'European Capital Integration', *B.B.R.*, November 1973

'When £3,000m is not £3,000m', *The Times*, 18 October, 1974

'Mr Healey still willing to wound but no longer afraid to strike', *The Times*, 13 November, 1974

'What future for the Stock Exchange?' *Sunday Telegraph*, 17 November, 1974

'Arab money: the real significance', *Sunday Telegraph*, 8 September, 1974

'Misconceptions about the stock market', *The Times*, 23 September, 1974

'Invisibles, a special report on the City of London', *The Times*, 9 October, 1974

'Finance for European industry', *The Times*, 16 April, 1973

'The cash flow crisis – £3,000m. gap', *Sunday Telegraph*, 22 September, 1974

'Healey must act to stop share slide', *Sunday Telegraph*, 18 August, 1974

'The crisis of confidence in the stock market', *The Times*, 19 August, 1974

'How the days of plenty in the City came to an end', *The Times*, 5 August, 1974

'The faint hearts of the Stock Exchange', *The Times*, 24 August, 1974.

'The crisis of cash for industry', *The Times*, 17 September, 1974

'A step in the right direction', *The Times*, 11 November, 1974

'New source of funds for industry', *The Times*, 13 November, 1974

'Long-term fund needed to stimulate investment by industry', *The Times*, 25 October, 1974

'Mr Slater prefers cash', *The Times*, 1 June, 1974

'Coping with industry's cash shortage', *Sunday Telegraph*, 20 October, 1974

'What it feels like to be hammered', *Sunday Telegraph*, 6 October, 1974

'Uncovering the men who run your pension fund', *Sunday Telegraph*, 19 May, 1974

'Stockbrokers on a tightrope', *The Times*, 2 April, 1974

'Green paper on company law reform: who should regulate the City?', *The Times*, 30 May, 1974

'Ironing out The Code anomalies', *The Times*, 6 June, 1974.

'Brothers deny "stagging" charges', *The Times*, 10 May, 1974

'Panel statement on St Martins-Hay's Wharf', *The Times*, 6 April, 1974

'Structure of Industry', Geoffrey Bone, *British Economy Survey*, Spring 1972

Bank of England Quarterly Bulletin, Vol. 14 No. 4

Economic Progress Report, No. 57, December 1974

'Regenerating industry', *The Economist*, 8 February, 1975

'Third time luckier', *The Economist*, 16 November, 1974

'Buckshot or bandages?' *The Economist*, 14 December, 1974

'Climb another mountain?' *The Economist*, 19 October, 1974

'Living with Harold again', *The Economist*, 19 October, 1974

'Investment: 1975 is the year . . .' *The Economist*, 15 February, 1975

'Rally in New York', *The Economist*, 15 February, 1975

'Guardian extra on indexing', *The Guardian*, 9 July, 1974.

'Stock profits: a business wonderland?' *The Times*, 7 November, 1974

'Who benefits from stock relief?', *Sunday Telegraph*, 17 November, 1974

'Shortcomings of inflation accounting as an answer to the cash crisis', *The Times*, 11 October, 1974

'Taking all things into account', *The Times*, 11 November, 1974

'A.B.C. of inflation accounting', *Sunday Telegraph*, 19 May, 1974

'Property: delicate issue for the Government', *The Times*, 13 December, 1974

'Taking stock of the jobbers', *The Times*, 22 November, 1977

'Few signs of a coherent acquisition strategy at the NEB', *The Times*, 8 May, 1977

'State enterprise: year one', *The Economist*, 7 May, 1977

'Investment in Britain. A survey', *The Economist*, 12 November, 1977

Treasury Economic Progress Report, February, 1977, December, 1977 and May, 1978

'Which way to a national securities market?' *The Economist*, 29 April, 1978

'End of an institutional era in the United States?' *The Times*, 23 November, 1977

'Club rules under fire', *The Economist*, 5 November, 1977

'The City's largest cartel', *The Economist*, 8 October, 1977

'Accountants and Inflation', W. T. Baxter, LBR, October, 1977

'Accountants funk inflation', *The Economist*, 2 July, 1977

'Profits and Inflation', *The Economist*, 4 December, 1976

'New issues maintain their momentum', MBR, September, 1978

'London chooses the wrong option', *The Economist*, 25 March, 1978

'Why the SEC pounced on option traders', *The Economist*, 22 October, 1977

Financial Journalism and Sources

Stock Exchange Official Year Book

Exchange Telegraph Co. Ltd

Bank of England Quarterly Bulletin

Barclays Bank Review

Lloyds Bank Review

Midland Bank Review

National Westminster Bank Review

The Investors Chronicle

The Financial Times

The Times

Sunday Times

The Economist

INDEX

For simplicity all shares are grouped under that head, and Taxation likewise under the head Taxation.

Accounts (of companies)
  appropriation, 12–13
  inadequacy of information from, 73
  inflation and the, 92–6
  profit and loss, *see* Profit and Loss Account
  trading, 12–13
  use of, to assess prospects, 11–14
Accounts (Stock Exchange), 52
Acts of Parliament
  Companies Act (1967), 32, 73
  Finance Act (1965), 47
  Finance Act (1977), 32
  Limited Partnership Act (1907), 2
Advance Corporation Tax, 30, 105
Articles of Association, 5
Assets, fixed and current, 5–7

Balance sheet, 3, 5–7, 73–4
  specimen of, 20
Bankruptcies, 100
Banks
  borrowing from West Germany, 68–70
  loans from, 3, 27–8, 29
  see also Merchant Banks
Bibliography, 136–8
Bills of Exchange, 29
'Blue Chips', 56
Bolton Committee, 31–2
Brokerage, commission on, 132
Brokers, 16, 76
  as fund raisers, 35

should not act as jobbers, 81–2
  see also under Stock Exchange, how it works
Budget, effect of 1974 measures in, 102–7

Call options, 55–6
Capital
  authorized, issued and paid-up, 5, 6, 7
  company's working, 21–2
  cover for debentures, 21–6
  funding by re-arrangement of, 43–5
  gearing ratio, 14–15, 23–6
  priority percentage, 23–4
  structure, specimen of, 15
Carry-over business, 57–8
Cash flow, 8, 103
Certificate of Incorporation, 5
Charterhouse Industrial Development Company, 33
City Capital Markets Committee (as to malpractice), 80–81
City Code on Take-overs and Mergers, *see* Take-overs
Companies
  Certificate of Incorporation, 5
  decline in profitability of, 89–102
    (*for detail see under Stock Exchange* (*Modern history of*))
  insolvency of, 1
  limited joint stock, 2–3, 4
  liquidation of, 1
  net current assets, 21–3

Companies – *cont.*
  progress of, effect on share prices, 53–4, 60–63, 83
  prospectus, 5
  public, 2–3
  Registrar of, 3, 5
  setting up, 4–5
  Stock Exchange guide to progress of, 60–63
  working capital, 21–2
  see also Small Firms; Taxation
Consideration, what is a?, 132
Contangos, 57
Contract Stamp Duty, 132
Cover, 22–7, 133
Credit
  financing by trade, 3, 29
  through hire-purchase, 30
Current Purchasing Power system, 95

Debentures, 3, 21–7
  and share compared, 27
  Corporation Tax and, 126–7
  to raise new issues, 37
Deflation measures, 98
Depreciation, 7–10, 84–6
Development Grants (NEB), 129
Dividend rate, formula for, 113
Dividends, 8, 17
  and new issues, 37
  see also Yield
Dividend Yield, *see* Yield

Earnings per share, 15
Economist, The, 57, 96, 106–7, 107–8
Economy, private sector of, 1–3
EEC, financial dealings with, 68–72
Equities, *see* Finance, self- and share-
Equity Capital for Industry Scheme, 33
European financial market dealings, 68–72

European Free Trade Area, 71–2
Export Credits Guarantee Department, 30–31
Exports, invisible earnings from, 66

Fair Trading, Office of, 81–2
FIFO stock system, 93
Finance
  self- and share-, 1–18
    business organization, three main types of, 1–3
    capital structure and share prospects, 14–15
    company accounts, use of, to assess prospects, 11–14
    depreciation funds, 8–10
    external, 3–8
    ordinary shares, 4
    preference shares, 4
    retained profits, 10–11
    role of, 1
    share finance resources, allocation of, 17–18
    Stock Exchange, finance through, 16–17
    see also Issuing Houses
  through loans, 19–34
    debentures, 21–7
    for small firms, 31–4
    long-term, 28
    short-term, 28–31
  see also Business Finance *under* Taxation; Issuing Houses
Finance Bills, 3, 29
Finance Corporation for Industry, 31, 33, 105–7
Finance Houses, 35
  see also Issuing Houses
Financial journals, names of useful, 139
Financial Times, The, 51, 133–5
Financial Times Industrial Ordinary Share Index, 87–8, 107–9

Financial Times Share Information Service, terms used in, explained, 133–5
Foreign exchange dealings, 66
Formulae to assess share performance, 113–15
Funding, *see* Brokers; Capital; Finance; Issuing Houses; Stock Exchange

Games involving mock investment, 132–5
Gearing ratio, 14–15, 23–6
General Index of Retail Prices, 95
Glossary of terms used in share purchases, 132–5
'Going Public', 36, 110
Good-will, 7, 21
Government policy
dividend restraint, 109–10
monetary restraint, 99–101
1974 Budgets, 102–7
prices and incomes, 96–7
Grants
development, 129
investment, 125, 127–8
Gresham Trust, 33

High/low of the year (shares), 133
Hire-purchase, 30

Industrial and Commercial Finance Corporation, 28, 31, 33, 105
Inflation, effects of, 92–6
Inside Dealing, 74, 77–8
Insolvency, 1
Insurance companies, investment by, 45–6
Interest, 3
see also Debentures; Yield
International Monetary Fund, 28
Investment allowances and grants, 125, 127–8
Investment Games, 132–5

Investment Trusts, 46–7
Investors Chronicle, The, 51, 123–4
Invisible earnings from exports, 66
Issuing Houses, 16, 35–47
advice of, as to type of security, 37
allocation of issues, 39–40
allotment letters, 39–40
by capital re-arrangement, 43–5
client, investigating, 35–6
failure of new flotations, 110
functions of, 35–40
insurance companies, 45–6
investment by Institutions, 45–7
investment trusts, 46–7
letters of entitlement, 42
methods available, 40
non-voting shares, 45
offer for sale, 40
over subscription, 38
pension funds, 46
placing, 40–41
pre-emption rule, 40
prospectus, 39–40
rate of the offer, how to decide, 37–8
rights issue, 42–3
scrip issues, 43–5
shares, nominal, par and no par, 38
specialist intermediaries, 45–7
striking price, 41
tenders, 40–41
under subscription, 38
underwriting, 39
unit trusts, 46
see also Stags *under* Stock Exchange (how it works)

Jobbers, 16, 76
should not act as brokers, 81–2
see also under Stock Exchange, how it works
Journals, financial, names of, 139

Keynes, John Maynard, 53–4

Letters of Allotment, 39–40
Letters of Entitlement, 42
Liabilities, current and share capital, 6–8
LIFO stock system, 93
Limited liability, 4
Liquidation, 1, 99
Liquidity problems, 90
Loans, *see under* Banks; Finance

Macmillan Committee, 31
Markets, bear- bull-, and prices, *see under* Stock Exchange
Memorandum of Association, 5
Merchant banks, 35, 47
Mergers, *see* Take-over bids
Moodies Services, 51
Moracrest Investments, 33–4
Morpeth Committee, 95–6

National Enterprise Board, 129–31
New Issue Market, *see* Issuing Houses
New York Stock Exchange, 75–7

Offers for sale (new issues), 40
Options
    put and call, 54–6
    traded, 56–7
Out of hours trading (on Stock Exchange), 82
Overdrafts, *see under* Banks

Pension Funds, investing, 46
Placing a new issue, 40–41
Price-earnings ratio, 113, 114
    shown in *Financial Times*, 133–4
Prices, fluctuation of market, 10
Prices and Incomes Policy, 96–7
Profit and Loss Account, 3, 9, 12–13, 73–4

Profits
    and trading account, 12
    decline in company, 89–102 (*for detail see under Stock Exchange* (*Modern history of*))
    effect on market value of, 11–12
    on Stock Exchange, 52–3
    Prices and Incomes Policy and, 96–7
    retained, 10–11, 84–6
    taxation on, 8
Proprietorships, 2
Prospectus, 5, 39–40
Publications, names of useful, 139
Put options, 55–6
'Put through' dealing, 82

Registrar of Companies, *see under* Companies
Retail Price Index, 95
Retained earnings, 10–11, 84–6
Rights issues, 15, 42–3

Scrip issues, 43–5
Self-finance, *see* Finance
Share-finance, *see* Finance
Shares
    convertible preference, 112
    cumulative preference, 111–12
    how to read *Financial Times* Share Information Service, 133–5
    measuring the performance of, 113–15
    ordinary, *see under* Finance; *Financial Times* Industrial Ordinary Share Index
    participating preference rights, 112
    preference, 111–12
        a case study in, 116–19
        non-cumulative, 111
        see also under Finance
    preferential, 112